MIDNIGHT SKIRMISH

When the grenading tapered off, Pfc. John Mucci saw a large North Vietnamese soldier loom directly in front of his foxhole, then dash toward him. Mucci went after him with an entrenching shovel, killing him by bashing in his head.

From the outer darkness came a mocking voice in English: "Hey GI, how is your company commander?"

"He's fine," Mucci sang out, undaunted. "How about yours?"

"Not very well. . . . You have just killed him."

WEST TO CAMBODIA

"Marshall is good at conveying the sense of astonishment and unreality that is combat."

—*Saturday Review*

Books by S.L.A. Marshall
from Jove

NIGHT DROP: THE AMERICAN
AIRBORNE INVASION OF NORMANDY

PORK CHOP HILL

WEST TO CAMBODIA

WEST TO CAMBODIA

S.L.A. MARSHALL
BRIGADIER GENERAL, USAR-RET.

INCLUDING SKETCHES BY THE AUTHOR

A JOVE BOOK

WEST TO CAMBODIA

A Jove Book / published by arrangement with
The Battery Press, Inc.

PRINTING HISTORY
Original edition published in 1968
The Battery Press edition published in 1984
Jove edition / December 1986

ISBN: 0-515-08890-0

Jove Books are published by The Berkley Publishing Group,
200 Madison Avenue, New York, N.Y. 10016.
The words "A JOVE BOOK" and the "J" with sunburst
are trademarks belonging to Jove Publications, Inc.

PRINTED IN THE UNITED STATES OF AMERICA

Contents

WEST TO CAMBODIA

Foreword————————

In early 1968 there was a fierce debate on Capitol Hill, which carried over into our national press and TV forums, then mushroomed into an international wrangle, with shouts of defiance and numerous maledictions before interest at last subsided.

The question: Should our forces fighting along the Cambodian border engage in hot pursuit when the enemy crossed into so-called neutral territory? Of course, Prince Sihanouk repeated then, as he had insisted all along, that the North Vietnamese Army made little or no use of his country. That is his fairy story, and our State Department perforce swallows it.

It was at that time that I went back over my field notes and verified what my memory told me—that the opportunity for hot pursuit into Cambodia virtually never arose. The debate, therefore, was much ado about nothing. But this is not unusual in war. People tend to get excited about the wrong things, and, though the facts of a matter may be incontrovertible, they militate little or none against heated opinions.

I know the Cambodian border country fairly well from having visited parts of it afoot, and from having flown its length several times in clear weather when observation was unlimited. I admit my fascination with this zone of operations in South Vietnam. To begin, it merely stirred my interest during the spring and early summer of 1966 because Brig. Gen. Glenn Walker was operating there with a task force suitably named TF Walker.

He kept it moving constantly and joined fairly close in screening operations. This, I believed, was the sound way of dealing with any real or fancied threat from the westward. Walker talked the same language in the brief time we had together when we were sore-pressed from quite different directions. He was using armor and infantry that moved in APC's.

Even this much later in the game, I could wish that Walker, an inveterate doughboy, had been boosted into a position where he might have said: "This is how we will counter and control NVA threats out of Cambodia; we will not get into knockdown, drag-out fights on ground where we yield the enemy every advantage."

I can remember Glenn at Landing Zone Oasis on a humid day in June, 1966. We had first met on a touch-down-and-skip visit when my old friend, Harry Kinnard, then commanding at corps, piloted the Huey onto the pad for a quick talk about the situation. Later, I flew back on my own to resume the conversation. It lasted perhaps about 40 minutes. All this time I was listening, for Glenn kept saying things worth hearing. His G-3, a nobleman, kept bringing us mugs of iced tea, for which I was grateful. Still, I remember Glenn's firm expression as he said the parting words: "You must come out here and lose yourself in it. Nothing west of Oasis is done easily. Out here, the advantage is all their way."

Being relatively sure that I was on my last visit to Oasis and would soon return home, I put his words into my field notebook only because it is a lifetime habit.

Six months thereafter, out of writing down the battle notes that I have here put in narrative form, I at last thoroughly understood what Glenn Walker, quite gently, was trying to say to me that much earlier.

Rattling around the Cambodian border held nothing good for our side except in the most extraordinary circumstances where sheer luck or some fluke made things break our way. The enemy, from out of the Cambodian base camps, was ever scouting, measuring, and plotting the countryside out beyond Oasis. He had every possible landing zone tabbed and taped and knew where to set his mortars to zero in on them. We were literally engaging the Charlies on the maneuver ground where they did their training exercises. Although we made numerous forays into the region, we never stayed very long, except for the Special Force soldiers assigned to lonely outposts such as Du Co. Our average line infantry unit was almost as foreign to the countryside as a first astronaut landing on the moon. The comparison may seem farfetched. Let him who thinks so read through these pages in search of even one vista that resembles anything familiar. I can remember only one place close to Cambodia that struck me as similar to landscape that I had long known. The trench of the Ia Drang River, a necklace of pools, cascades, and white water freshing through solid rock, is uncommonly like Ontario's French River. It is strange that any countryside so lovely can also be deadly. To walk or fly about there during an autumn twilight is to find oneself in a place seemingly as remote from man as the Arctic tundra. In the wet season, around May and June, it is one vast lagoon; during the winter dry spell, it is a waste of lush grass, rock-ribbed hills, and red earth.

I marveled that, mystified as our young foot soldiers were by many things in the environment, surprised, tricked, and trapped repeatedly by an enemy whose tactical stratagems were truly quite limited in number, they still carried on with such little complaint and fought with so much quiet courage. Each of these fights is reported in its entirety. Nothing has been deleted or cleaned up. The language used is as the cast of characters recalled it, though there is remarkably little profanity or obscenity. The mistakes are numerous, and they were discussed without restraint by all ranks; there was always the hope that other men would profit thereby. What is missing altogether is any showing of slackness, wavering, or cowardice in moments of crisis. There is never panic. No one runs from the fight or tries to pull a sneak. The greater the pressure, the more helpful they become to one another. They seem almost too good for the country that sent them forth, a country that took little interest in the nature of their ordeal and was for the most part indifferent to their welfare.

None is a number or a file to me. I knew them; and some of them I got to know very well. I can recall their faces and their voices. Later, when the special word was sent me that this one, or the other one, was killed in another fight later along, it hit home no less hard than when 50 years ago I first lost men out of my own platoon. One may never get used to such things, any more than to the indecency and impudence of those critics of the war whose attack is so envenomed as to spread the impression through the nation that its fighting sons are engaging in something completely dishonorable. I am sure the reader will find character imprinted on every page of this book, but it did not shape up from the influence of our colleges. Our average soldier over there is a high school graduate. Of the hundreds of officers and men who passed through my hands, only two had done post-graduate work at a university.

Their wholehearted cooperation as witnesses made the book possible. The source materials are all in my home, though copies of the raw data are in use at the Pentagon. My wife, Cate, serves as my Girl Friday, doing all of the cross-checking, suggesting, and editing. And, bless her, she is also a first-class cook.

S. L. A. Marshall
Brig. Gen. USAR-Ret.

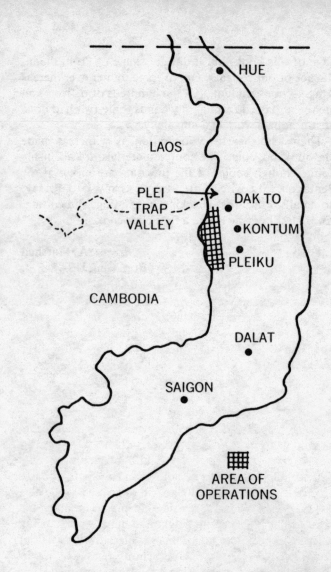

Map of Vietnam south of the 17th parallel, with area of operations along border with Cambodia indicated by cross-hatching. Arrow points to Plei Trap Valley.

A Small Elite————
————of Service

From the beginning, his superiors in Special Forces had told him firmly that he was too old for the kind of work he wished to do, and he continued to answer still more vehemently that age was the main thing in his favor, until at last he wore them out.

So it was perhaps inevitable that Sgt. 1st Cl. Normal A. Doney, 38, of Hammond, Ore., would have his way. What he wanted was a chance to make a big killing deep in enemy country with the aid of one other American and a pinch of Vietnamese—four to be exact.

"Let me tell you," he said time and again, "that these Viets do not listen to young Americans. But they'll go with somebody who has been around." That meant Doney, who had spent two years in Laos, and, because his way of putting it brisked and bristled with confidence, he in turn won it, both from the chiefs who had to give in and the Indians who had to go out.

His words and purpose aside, the man is anything but spectacular. Of medium height and quite average build, a little on the plump side, Doney is blessed with a face of such quiet mien and inconspicuous features that he would have no trouble losing himself in any crowd.

Once the idea was approved, he and Sgt. 1st Cl.
Charles L. Harper of Smyrna Beach, Fla., knew exactly
what to do. Their services had been requested by First
Brigade of the 25th Infantry Division, which would be
operating in the same general area out of Song Be to the
north of Tae Ninh.

First, the quartet of Vietnamese (the oldest was 30,
the youngest 23), consistent with standing procedure,
went into isolation behind barbed wire. Toward doubly
securing security, the six-man force would not get
together and talk over the task until one hour before the
pay run started. This was well understood by 1st Lt. Vu
Man Thong, the commander. It sat well enough with the
team sergeant, the corporal, and the lone private. They
simply complied with what their two "advisers" advised. The corporal was the hard rock of the lot, an old
hand with whom Doney had worked several times, a soldier he reckoned "would stick to the last." Only the
lieutenant spoke English. However, if he happened to
get killed, the team would be carrying SOI (standing operating instructions) cards, with side-by-side sentences
in the two essential languages covering everything that
need be said, and so communicating could continue.

On 15 August, 1966, in full daylight, Doney and
Harper made their only reconnaissance, flying by Huey
to the Cambodian border. They were looking particu-
larly for possible landing zones and E & E (escape and
evasion) routes. Doney spotted three LZ's (landing
zones) suitable to the mission and came away satisfied.
The E & E traces he viewed only as possible guidelines to
enemy locations. The team had no intention of moving
by trail even if things went wrong. So reflecting, the two
Americans flew back to Song Be to go over their plan
with the staff there. If what they hoped for eventually,
they would need a great deal of help from the people at

the base, and it must come quickly, unerringly.

In late afternoon of 16 August the six men formed and talked for the first time. Shortly before dusk, they flew. "Just one thing to remember," Doney said quietly to the pilot. "I want to be set down at last light. When there's barely light enough for you to see the ground and get away, that's it."

Their chosen spot was exactly three and one-half kilometers, a little more than two miles, due east of where a 35-foot-wide creek, flowing westward, joins the Dak Huit River at the Cambodian border. In picking the creek bank, Doney guided on what he thought was the best possible sign strung out for almost that same distance above the far shore of the stream. There the tropical forest rose to 100 feet or more. A far wind was blowing from the east. Hanging over the treetops like a mantle, he had noted as they flew eastward, was a thin layer of smoke that ended at the point chosen for their descent. Until then they had no hunches; they merely looked for a sign.

"So I knew they were there," said Doney, "but there was so much smoke it gave me second thoughts."

The Huey touched down at exactly 1905 onto a pad of tall elephant grass interlaced with vines, a soft cushion touched so lightly that the metal hardly made an imprint; the chopper was off and gone from the spot (coordinates YU217-346) in less than 10 seconds. Brief as was that grass-level hover, the six men did not see the takeoff. They were off instantly, running in the direction of the already plotted recon, the team sergeant acting as point, the private playing tail gunner at the rear, Doney midway in the formation, carrying the command radio, a PRC-25.

It was like a bending race; they zigzagged from the start, though it was just a 50-meter sprint, about 55

yards, straight into the heavy stuff, where a tall stand
of bamboo and some towering mahoganies completed
their isolation.

They sat there for 10 minutes, breathing hard while
the dark closed, and they were happy to see it come. The
long wait had a purpose. They wanted to get the roar of
the chopper out of their ears so that their hearing would
be keen. It took five minutes. Then they listened but
heard nothing save the rushing waters of the turbulent
creek. Not a word was spoken. When came time to
move, they coordinated with hand signals.

Now walking carefully, they moved east 100 meters
at a sharp angle toward the creek bank, reversed
themselves and followed along the bank for the same
distance, moved uphill with backs to the stream for
another 100 meters, went westward through the bush,
which took about 15 minutes, and returned to their
starting point.

By then, Doney and Thong were both satisfied that
their arrival had gone undetected and that no one was
moving toward them. So they prepared to settle for the
night. They had found a roughly crescent-shaped briar
patch, the ends of which tied into a thick clump of bamboo, leaving an open space between the two horns of the
crescent.

It was ideal bivouac ground for them. They sat down,
backs together, feet outward, hands joined, so that they
formed a small, closely knit circle from which each man
looked outward. It was in this formation that they
passed the next eight hours, a sit-in of warriors pat-
terned after a Quaker meeting. Not a word or a cough
interrupted the jungle silence; if anyone came, if any
question was to be asked, they would communicate with
hand pressure. They hungered, but no one thought of
eating; in fact, they had brought no food. As for smok-

ing, these men had long since cut out the use of tobacco, claiming it dulls the sense of smell, even as speaking little tends to sharpen hearing.

Occasionally some member of the circle would drop off into a doze. That was permissible, so long as he didn't snore and so long as the circle of hands remained unbroken. They were well coated with repellent; had it not been so, the infestation of tree leeches would have made their prolonged vigil impossible.

Even so, to average ears, the story of their night sounds like an unendurable strain. They, on the other hand, insist it was not so, philosophizing that the locked circle of human companionship exalts the spirit and makes the worst misery tolerable.

About 0200 a little rain fell and Doney, seeing a few low clouds scudding westward, felt worried for the first

Map shows the security movements made after landing by Sgt. 1st Cl. Normal A. Doney of Special Forces and the team that he led into enemy territory.

time. Without good visibility soon after first light, his mission was dead. Shortly thereafter the sky cleared.

At 0400 they all came head-up alert and the circle was broken. Of a sudden, from across the creek, they could hear much chattering and coughing. Then the chatter was drowned out by a clatter, as of sticks being banged together. Though the rhythm was marimbalike, Doney thought he knew what it meant. These were signal sticks. From his own side of the stream he could hear an answer beaten out. Not being able to read the signals, he closed his mind to the phenomenon.

At first light, which came more than an hour later, Doney made up his first spot report. He knew that his FAC (forward air controller), according to plan, would be in the skies somewhere near him at sunup. His instructions for the FAC had been: "At first light you must come no nearer than one mile from me and you must keep flying on a north-south line."

Lieutenant James Flanagan, the FAC, kept the rendezvous to perfection. As the sun came just high enough to bathe the clearing upstream from their hideout in the bramble and briar, Doney saw a plane flying at about 1,000 feet. It was a mile to the east, flying north to south. He had just time enough to dash to the clearing and catch the sunlight in a hand mirror, angled toward the plane. By extraordinary luck, Flanagan caught the gleam immediately.

"Wait until you give me a fix," Doney said to him over the PRC-25. "I have two messages for you."

Working from the same map as Doney, Flanagan made a quick calculation based on where he had seen the mirror flash, and pinpointed the party's location. Of that precaution came the second extraordinary break. The Huey pilot of the night before had given Doney a fix, and it was dead wrong, being 1,500 meters east of his location. The correction was just in time. This happened at 0715.

Doney then told Flanagan about the smoke that he had seen rising from directly across the creek. The strike should come in where the smoke first appeared above the treetops.

As his second item of business, he told Flanagan, "As the strike comes in, we will already be moving east. We should be picked up about 500 meters from here, next to the creek bank."

And that, really, is what he thought he was going to do, for want of any better laid plan.

But while he talked to Flanagan, and even as the clamor from across the creek rose higher, the Vietnamese team sergeant had wandered down to the edge of the water to have a closer look. While Doney was saying to the FAC, "I want the strike brought in now," the little Viet was gasping at a spectacle that transformed the entire operation from a hit-or-miss thing into a blast.

He was back in a minute panting out the big news. And he shook all over as he blurted it out. It was the first time Doney had even seen him at such a pitch of excitement.

"It's PT [physical training]," he said. "They're going through exercises. More than a hundred of them. Close together. Right out in the open. Those sticks you hear. No signals. They beat it out to establish rhythm. It was just 75 meters away. I could have hit them with a rock."

Doney got Flanagan on the radio. "Never mind the smoke," he said. "There's a VC mob in the open. Get it. Give me a couple of minutes. I gotta move another 100 meters off."

But Doney and party didn't win that extra margin of

safety for two reasons, the first being that the strike came in too fast. Three jets were already barreling toward them as they started, and the jets were flying very low. Still, the running men had moved 50 meters to the south, and the big whammy had not yet splattered the north bank with blood, rubble, and dust, when Doney, running first, stopped, held out his arms, and stayed the party.

The six men hit earth just as the first bombs exploded across the creek. But that was not what impelled them. Directly to their fore and not more than 75 meters away, Doney saw more smoke—a great swatch of it—stretching out westward above the canopy of the forest. And in that same flash instant before he pitched headlong to earth, just as the bombs went off, his eyes beheld a number of khaki-clad figures darting about amid the scrub and tree trunks. It was the camp of another NVA (North Vietnamese Army) company on their side of the creek. The six men had been so preoccupied with the prospect to north of them ever since first light, that none had bothered to look, much less scout, toward the south.

So they hugged earth, and they were so shaken for those few moments when their noses were in the dirt, that they could not think. The ground lying between them and the fresh menace was quite flat and wide open save for patches of elephant grass. It seemed inconceivable that their rush southward had gone unobserved. That meant they were trapped. Doney knew he had to do something. For lack of any more constructive idea, he looked at his watch. The time was 0730.

Within those seconds, while the party lay flattened and motionless, the three jets made their perfect kill north of the creek. It was a total surprise, possibly assisted by the noise and enthusiasm of the stick-banging,

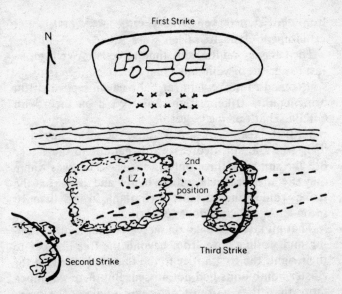

The three air strikes directed by Doney, the first against the enemy camp, the others against fleeing troops.

which dulled the warning sound of the low-level approach until too late. Caught in the open, still exercising, the enemy were hit first by napalm, then bombs, then CBU's (cluster bomb units). It was a slaughter grim and great. Where men had been, the brush-sprinkled flat was now ablaze.

Doney and his mates now heard loud screaming from that direction. It was their only impression, for they did not look back. Head up, peering forward, Doney saw that the foreground was bare of skirmishers. Not one enemy soldier had left the tree line to move toward him. It was a wonderful relief, the one bit of encouragement he needed to get going again.

He was on the PRC-25, speaking to Flanagan again: "There's a new target. Another company. Within the tree line, 125 meters south of where we were last night.''

"Got it," Flanagan said.

Then Doney added, this time in code, "We'll move east to get out of your way."

"You can't move very far," Flanagan replied. "I'm bringing the strike in right now. We'll hit them with CBU's. That's all we've got."

With the team sergeant leading, the men jumped to their feet and sprinted eastward, parallel to the creek. But the run took them only 75 meters. That was where they saw the three jets coming in low and knew that the strike would land just off their flank in less than 10 seconds. Again, they dove for earth.

That hit also was dead on target. A chorus of screaming and wailing rose from beyond the tree line off to their right, the first notice to the flattened men that the cluster bomb units had not missed. But there was much more than that. Groups of enemy soldiers, fleeing in panic from the woods, dashed past them, one group of three striding within five feet of Doney. If they saw him, it made no impression, such was their terror. Still, it startled Doney that they had not even stopped to shed their packs. And there were more men in khaki coming.

Doney had again signaled his position to Flanagan with the hand mirror. "You've got to bring in another strike," he said. "Get it closer to us."

"I don't dare," Flanagan answered. "That last one was much too close."

"You don't understand," Doney argued. "They're overrunning us. If you can't lay on one between us and the wood, then give us a strike to the east."

This time when the jets came on, AK-47 rifles and machine guns fired on them from out of the wood. Had the same weapons been turned against Doney and his crew, that would have been a dismal end to the saga.

But they were leading a charmed life.

Doney got the others formed in perimeter; at least that is what he called it. What he meant was that the six men deployed in a circle about 15 feet across, heads outward, feet inward, bodies flattened on perfectly flat ground that was shorn of hummocks, tree stumps, or anything else that might protect them. These men were not wearing steel helmets; the "pots" are too noisy and also interfere with hearing. Instead they had soft fatigue hats of camouflage cloth. But there were three other radios in the party besides Doney's PRC-25.

"Put your radios in front of your head," Doney said to them. "That will give you a little cover if they come on shooting."

It was a grain of comfort for Doney and three others; two of them weren't helped a bit.

Now Doney was on his radio, talking to Flanagan in code, and, if possible, this time there was more urgency in his voice than ever before. "You got to yank us," he said. "Put the word out 'Emergency.' We can't stay on here."

"I will do what I can," Flanagan said, but he was no longer in position to do very much. His pilot had just told him that the ship was running out of gas.

So, emergency or not, between one thing going wrong and another, the men had to stay as they were for the better part of an hour. To add to their sweating, they belatedly noted that a wide trail that came out of the tree line and jogged eastward parallel to the creek had its turning within a rod of their circle. Otherwise, the day could not have been more beautiful. A few fleecy clouds lent but a touch of contrast to the bluest sky they had ever seen. The sun beat down but the temperature was mild. So it was not hot; to them, it only seemed that way.

By the time the tac air ships had departed the scene and Flanagan ran out of gas, the Army relay (communications) Huey was overhead. So they felt that much better for having a little friendly company within eyesight, though they were very thirsty and hungering. A brief appearance was also put in by the C & C (command and control) ship of the 25th Division under a Major Luttrell, who tarried just long enough to say, "Got to go now; we're running out of gas."

"So am I," Doney replied.

But he wasn't quite. For there remained one special mission, which he took unto himself. If they were to make a quick rendezvous with the Huey pilot when he finally came in for the extraction, he would have to have a mark. So tucking a cerise panel under his arm, Doney crawled off a hundred meters or so through the elephant grass to place the panel on the LZ where they had set down the night before. During this labored passage, which killed at least 30 minutes, he saw no sign that the enemy was moving toward his men. But then a man crawling headdown through elephant grass doesn't see very far.

As he got back to the circle, three slicks (copters) covered by three gunships (rocket-firing Hueys) roared in at treetop level to strafe the ground where tac air had put on the first two strikes. Doney and his men started crawling toward the cerise panel, figuring that the attack was aimed to beat down the enemy just prior to the arrival of the rescue chopper.

That guess was on the nose. Crawling, Doney got the word from the pilot who would lift them out: "Get ready—I'm coming in."

By then both gunships were under intense fire from machine guns on both sides of the creek. Doney saw them lurch as they took hit after hit, though they didn't go down.

"Don't come in," Doney said to the pilot. "There's way too much fire."

The pilot kept right on coming. The six men could see the Huey now. It was just over the trees south of the creek where the second air strike had exploded. Missing the cerise panel altogether, and also missing a large bomb crater by not more than three feet, the pilot touched down within 50 meters of Doney and his men.

They were already up and running as fast as they could. The Vietnamese team sergeant outran them all by at least five lengths, though he broke trail through the elephant grass all the way. Doney, the last man aboard, cocked his thumb high in the "go" sign before sinking into a seat.

"Give my gunners a target!" the pilot yelled.

"Shucks," grinned Doney, "tell them to shoot any-where."

Before he could get the words out, they were up and winging away and both door gunners were firing like mad. Fire was coming against them from all around the circle, and at least three machine guns were blasting with tracers from the far side of the creek.

From above them, where the Army relay ship orbited, a doleful voice came at them through the headsets: "You'll never make it! You'll never make it!"

They completely failed to believe the dirge. They had had so much luck all along that it could not break now. The takeoff was at exactly 0945. There were 23 fresh bullet holes in the Huey when it got to home base less than 40 minutes later. No one aboard had been hit or hurt.

At 1400 on the same day Doney returned by Huey to

reconnoiter the scene of the action. North Vietnamese soldiers swarmed all over the area. The craft dropped lower to check on what was happening. These were fresh troops, apparently. Some were setting up gun positions. Others were dragging bodies to the creek bank. Doney called in another air strike. Minutes later he saw men and weapons vanish in the air as the bombs exploded.

Later that evening, at about an hour before sunset, he flew again to the creek for a final look. Along the bank next to where he had been that morning was moored a cortege of about 50 sampans, preparing to carry the dead and wounded back to Cambodia. He did not call for another strike; he silently reckoned that he and his mates had racked up the greater part of an NVA battalion. It was enough for one day.

The tale would keep to tell his children some day. There were two of them in the family home at Fayetteville, N.C., both infants. The youngest he had not yet seen.

The Sweet,————————
————————Sweet Smell

Alpha Company (1/12th) of the Fourth Infantry Division, by the dawn of 26 October, 1966, had been threshing about in the boondocks of the far western Central Highlands of South Vietnam for 36 days, accomplishing nothing except its own physical hardening.

The troops were so accustomed to searching diligently to find nothing that it was regarded as SOP for the course. The conviction made them no happier. It was beautiful countryside, but the going was all either up or down, and soldiers too soon wearied of tramping endlessly over hills and ridges.

Fourth Division, under the command of Maj. Gen. Arthur Collins, was not only the latest newcomer to the Army in Vietnam but, in one respect, the most uncertain quantity. The earlier birds had been more or less old-line outfits, with a preponderance of made soldiers, if not veterans from earlier wars. Before staging out of Fort Lewis, Wash., Collins had fleshed out his division with draftees. Throughout all units, the conscripts were heavily in the majority.

Until this time, the division had experienced a nigh bloodless debut, a fact that neither burdened nor cheered the men of Lt. Brendan T. Quann's company when they started marching early that morning from the hill where they had bivouacked. Their concern was that they were spinning their own wheels. The column counted 121 men. As to what they knew of their mission, most of them could have replied to the question with the lines from "Paint Your Wagon": "Where'm I goin'? I don't know . . . When will I get there? I ain't certain. All I know is I am on my way!"

They were headed northwest. That was because the forward air controller had gone over the map with Quann, pointed his finger at a pimple on it, and said, "I think if you make that, it will serve as an LZ." As small a thing as this determined their direction of march, which was not untypical of search operations in that remote, completely strange countryside; it may be likened to seeking a needle in a haystack.

Leading the march was First Platoon under a 27-year-old second lieutenant, Ronald C. Weindel, of Alton, Ill., who had attended Southern Illinois University. His outfit did not stay long in the van. They were in thick jungle, so thick that it called for steady hacking with machetes; to take the hard labor, the platoons had to be rotated to the fore. By 1300 they had advanced only 600 meters from where they had shoved off.

And there they stopped. After wading through a clean-flowing creek, they had come to a small knoll that was partly clear. A narrow footpath ran from the water to the rise. In the center of the path, Weindel saw four fresh banana peels. There were no other signs around the peels, such as footprints. Only the peels gave them pause; it meant people about, and not far away.

While they halted, other men brought Spec. 4 Joe Gentile forward to see Quann. Coming through the creek, Gentile had slipped on a rock and sprained an ankle so badly that he could not even hobble along. Quann looked him over and decided that he had to be evacuated. During the examination, other men moved off the trail to look around. One was back shortly, saying, "Several guys have crapped out there—not our guys—but it's fresh."

Quann made up his mind; this was the place to settle for the night. There was no viable landing zone in sight, which meant there was no chance for resupply. But they had some leftover rations. Gentile could be hauled aloft by an evac ship.

As a result of these coincidences, the company made camp on the nameless knoll at coordinates YA-726-530, next to the stream they dubbed, not very imaginatively, Rocky Creek. Quann had called the battalion S-3 (operations officer), Capt. Paul Freeman, to ask permission to stay there. Freeman at first objected strongly, then said lugubriously, "Well, OK, I'll take your body count in the morning."

There was much clearing to be done of the heavy brush all about, so the riflemen set to, with their machetes. The many tree stumps were blown by an engineer squad from Bravo of the 4th, with Sergeant Doyle in charge. Finally, they made a tracing of the night perimeter around the base of the knoll, which ran about 40 by 70 by 40 meters. The earth at the base was loose enough, and the foxholes were dug waist deep. It was not quite a picnic, but there were similarities.

At 1400 Quann set forth two squad-size patrols, one to prowl northeast, the other southwest. "Find out what you can," he told them, "but don't get into a fight." A good trail flanked the creek as it ran northeast to southwest, a condition that fixed the assignment. They took off in opposite directions. The two patrols were back in the perimeter by 1730, each having covered 1,000 meters or more without discovering anything new or interesting.

Meanwhile, the rest of the outfit had bathed and washed equipment and clothing in Rocky Creek. The day was clear and sunny, the water inviting, and, as Weindel put it, "After so many days of finding nothing but scenery, we were a complacent lot."

One Huey arrived in late afternoon to carry out Gentile. The helicopter proved, to everyone's astonishment, that it could use a few feet of the creek bank for a pad. Furthermore, it had C-rations aboard, and so they dined plentifully.

By dark, which came about 1830, the men were settled in. As fighting supplies go in Vietnam operations, they were not overarmed. The riflemen averaged about 400 rounds apiece for their M-16's, with two fragment grenades and six of smoke per man, a slight imbalance. There were 800 rounds for each of the M-60 machine guns. Loads for the M-79 gunners varied between 28 and 60. Each foxhole was armed with at least one claymore mine. There were 20 HE (high explosive) rounds for the one 81-mm. mortar.

Quann had ordered that one man would stay awake at each position and do a one-hour trick before waking his relief. This held for the main perimeter as well as for the four listening posts, one of which was posted to the fore of each platoon. On this matter Quann had some positive ideas: the LP's had to be way, way out, or there was no point in having them. The men grumbled, but that's how it was done.

The full moon, up early, bathed the landscape in clear light. Observation for night operations could not have been better.

Long after chow, and only a few minutes before they tucked in, three of the leaders sat talking about the possibilities of getting hit that night.

In the council were Weindel, 1st Sgt. Robert E. Crouse, and S.Sgt. William T. Akerley. The oldest soldier present, Akerley, who was 44, was also the most seasoned combat veteran. A Boston University man from Quincy, Mass., he had served with the 27th Division in World War II.

"I don't think an attack will come," Akerley said. "They're here, but they'll head for the high ground rather than fight us in the open."

"Hear the voice of experience," Weindel answered. "I'll take off my boots and helmet and that's all. Those signs bug me."

"I'm with you," said Crouse.

Soon the camp slept. Until midnight the night was quiet but for the usual, mournful jungle noises.

The salvation of this unit, and the frustrating of the North Vietnamese that night, may be reduced to one factor, simple, yet audacious: the company's listening posts had been thrown out 200 meters from the perimeter. LP's are without doubt safer at that distance, and the listeners have a better chance of survival than if they are deployed in a tight circle. There are several reasons for this. The greater radius gives each post more chance of going undetected in an attack that usually presses along one line. At that distance, the attackers are still formed in column. Furthermore, an American can usually outrun any Asian. To get back to the main position, the listener should run at a right angle to the line of the attack for some distance before cutting back. These are simple tactical principles, yet such is human nature that most of the time they are resisted in favor of the fanciful security that derives from being close to one's fellows.

To the men in the company LP's that night, it could hardly have seemed that they had been thrown way out on a limb. They did not react nervously.

Specialist 4 John H. Skorupa was a listener far out from First Platoon's sector. Skorupa, a 23-year-old Chicagoan educated at Western Illinois University, is a soldier with much phlegm in his system. His mate was Pfc. Yenson L. "Buck" Herron, 20, a high school dropout from Campbellsville, Ky. They got along famously.

At 2340 Skorupa made his final call over the RT (radio telephone) to report: "Everything negative." Then he wakened his relief, Herron, saying, "Your time now," and was almost instantly asleep. Five minutes later, Herron nudged him with his elbow. "Easy now," Herron whispered. "I see a VC."

Herron's ears had first picked it up—the faintest sound, as of one object scraping another. He looked back over his left shoulder. Ten meters away he saw a human head thrusting forward atop a pile of logs. The head was clearly profiled against the moonlit sky. In that moment the possibility of sudden death ceased being as remote as it had seemed in base camp.

By the time Skorupa looked, the first head had disappeared. Another head came up from behind the logs and the body began wiggling along the top of the pile.

First getting his M-16 in hand, Skorupa wakened Pfc. George Baco, a 22-year-old Canadian born in Quebec. The enemy soldier slithered down the pile of logs and dropped off the end, moving toward the perimeter. Skorupa was certain for that moment that the listening post had not been spotted. But he was afraid to use the RT; he figured there were other Charlies beyond the log pile and they would certainly hear. The Americans were squatted in heavy shadow.

But they were also unprotected. Skorupa nudged Herron and Baco and they all crawled about three yards to their right to get closer to the logs. They raised their

M-16's, ready to fire. From the far end of the log pile, an enemy voice cried, "Don't shoot, GI!" The slight sound of a bolt action had given the position away. Skorupa said, "Let 'em have it!" They all fired. It was good; the body of that one soldier was found there next morning.

Perhaps three seconds later they heard a mortar firing, not far away.

Skorupa now knew that the jig was up. "We got to get the hell out," he said. Then it came to him in a flash that he had left the radio at the original position. In the excitement, he had forgotten all about the instrument. It was too late to crawl back; from beyond the log pile came a great chatter of many voices. "Never mind the RT," he said.

At first they scuttled along on all fours to get out without showing too much body. Then it was up-and-go-fast-man in a hunched-over straight run along the trail, as speedily as they could haul out—"a world's record," Skorupa said, "for that kind of travel." No fire came after them, but there was one incident. Almost home, they had to scamper across a dew-soaked log that bridged a shallow ravine. Herron slipped, fell into the ravine, and lost his helmet when he landed headfirst. They waited for him to come up, gave him their hands and a big yank. As he joined them, Baco asked, "Where's your pot?" Herron started back, but Skorupa grabbed him, saying, "To hell with your pot—come along."

More quickly than it takes to tell it, they folded back into a half-alerted camp. Skorupa thought there was no need to report what had happened or to suggest what might come of it: their fire and the answering mortar had served notice.

Three mortar rounds had exploded just outside the

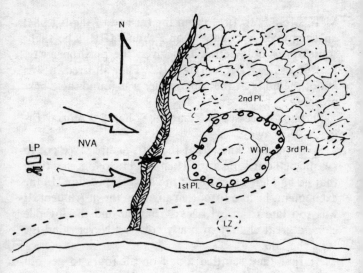

Enemy thrust around listening post (LP) and against Alpha Company's platoons.

perimeter while they were making it home. One fragment had smashed in the bridge of Sergeant Akerley's nose. As that round hit, Lieutenant Weindel awakened suddenly, yelling, "Oh God, let's go! Where's that God-damned mortar coming from?"

Weindel's yell awakened S.Sgt. Robert F. Wright, a soldier doing his fifth hitch. Wright was in position to take a good look before the second mortar round exploded. He saw the flash as the round came from the tube. He judged that the mortar was based about 200 meters west-northwest of the camp.

Wright yelled to Weindel, "There it is, sir!" and pointed. The enemy mortarman was obliging. He fired the third round and then Weindel saw the flash. Wright called to the nearest machine gunner, Pfc. Charles Marbury, "Go to work on that target and give it hell." Marbury swung his M-60 around and opened fire.

Then Weindel yelled, "Has our LP been called back?"

Somebody answered, "No."

"Cease fire!" Weindel called.

At that moment Weindel heard a hearty call from Skorupa: "LP coming in, sir, all OK."

As the three men stopped, greatly winded, Baco gasped, "Sir, they're all over the place."

It was Weindel's first knowledge that an infantry attack was coming on.

"Get in your foxholes," the lieutenant ordered. "By the way, where's the radio?"

A little shamefaced, Skorupa said, "We had to leave it out there."

It was Weindel's time to say, "Oh shit!"

Skorupa got in his last word to Akerley: "You might take note that that mortar is on a 320 azimuth." It was a nice, scholarly touch, an obvious suggestion, fully appreciated.

Akerley passed along Skorupa's tip to Lt. Michael F. Eastwood, commanding Heavy Weapons Platoon, and Weindel got on the RT to Eastwood to say, "Hey, get firing."

Just then, after firing three rounds, and before it possibly could have been hurt, the enemy's 82-mm. ceased action.

Skorupa, the thinker, already wedged in his foxhole with his two mates, called the turn, telling Herron, "That mortar made a mistake. It was supposed to wait the sounds of rifle fire, signaling that the VC infantry had closed. When we fired, that triggered the mortar.

And their rifles were too far back. Now what do they do?''

The mortar lull lasted all of six minutes. By then the enemy infantry had just entered the ravine where Baco had lost his helmet.

The six-minute pause was a two-way break for the camp. The men were busier than bird dogs. Weindel, who was without a radio, Skorupa having lost his only PRC-25, sent Crouse running to the CP (command post) to borrow one from Quann. The garrison's one 81-mm. mortar had not been dug in, but was resting on the open ground without a base plate. Eastwood turned the tube about and got it into action. The forward artillery observer, 2nd Lt. Calvin Dukes (A/4/42nd), had registered a number of fires in the late afternoon, though all in the wrong directions. He spent no time lamenting that. Within five adjustments he had the rounds falling where they were needed.

When the mortaring resumed, there were now two 82's going, one from the west-northwest, the other from the southwest. Eastwood snuffed out the first mortar with three rounds. It took Dukes a little longer, perhaps 10 minutes, to KO the second tube, this before any real damage had been done.

The ravine was about 30 meters forward from Weindel's foxhole. Over that distance he could hear Vietnamese voices jabbering loudly. The noise had already stirred S.Sgt. William F. Cherrington, who led Second Squad. His men crawled forward, grenading and laying down enough M-16 fire that the Vietnamese could not pop out of the ravine. Elsewhere around the perimeter men waited until they could see someone moving or could catch a muzzle flash. Then they fired. It was not easy; the elephant grass between the foxhole line and the ravine was eight feet high. Even so, not one enemy soldier got close to the defenders.

By the time the fight had been going 30 minutes, Dukes had brought his 105-howitzer fire back to the ravine and the shells were breaking just beyond the perimeter. It was the best kind of target line. The ditch was about 15 feet deep, with slightly more width than that, and the banks had a 45-degree slope. The enemy must not have known the ravine was there, and, once in it, could not get out, because the shelling directed by Lieutenant Dukes was sealing off the ends. Instead of affording protection like a trench, the ravine was a trap.

From about 75 meters off to the right of the perimeter, an enemy heavy machine gun went into action, atop the ravine bank. Pfc. George K. Adams engaged it with his M-60 machine gun and Pfc. Joseph G. Barnard with his M-79 grenade launcher. The enemy gun was dead within 15 seconds.

By 0230 Quann was worrying only about his ammunition supply. He passed around the word: "Take it easy. Don't fire until you have to. Everything is coming our way."

Until then, all the fire pressure had fallen against Weindel's sector only.

Quann moved there to ask Weindel, "Where are they? From the CP I get no real sense of it."

Weindel pointed out the far bank of the ravine. Six or seven—and possibly more—automatic rifles were blazing away from the other side, but the aim was very erratic.

"I think it's just a covering fire," Weindel said. "Their whole effort from now on is directed toward getting bodies and wounded out of the ditch."

On these terms, the fighting flickered for another hour and then faded out. The enemy grenading had long since ceased. Toward the close, the Americans could hear much moaning and screaming from within the ditch and beyond, but the danger was gone. The condition from there on was one of stabilized tension.

Quann set forth to look over his casualties. Sgt. Carl R. Harris had been hit by a bullet that broke his right shoulder. Pfc. George Alexander had taken a small grenade frag in his right shoulder, a simple flesh wound. And that was all.

At 0300 the moon went down and so did all weapons. When day broke, Skorupa and Wright took their squads and reconnoitered to the front. They found 21 dead North Vietnamese within the ravine. One wounded enemy soldier was made prisoner. Another Charlie, unhurt, stood in the wood lot beyond, waving a white shirt in token of surrender. They let him.

The healthy POW had a story to tell, and it came out about like this: "We were supposed to hit with a three-prong, three-company attack. One company couldn't get up there because of the ditch. The other two were driven back by your artillery."

Quann felt very pleased with himself. So did Dukes.

That afternoon Skorupa took his squad on another long patrol to the westward. He picked up another wounded Charlie from behind a rock. The patrol found much commo (communication) wire running along the trail. It led them to three large bamboo hootches (huts), which they tried to demolish. There were blood trails all around the buildings and the area was ringed with foxholes. On his return, as the platoon passed the familiar log pile, Skorupa remarked, "That's where I ceased being a boy."

Two hours later Weindel took all of First Platoon on a sweep over the same ground. On getting to the housing area, Weindel and Skorupa found that an enemy party had in the meantime visited there, collected the knocked-down walls of the huts, and neatly arranged them as overhead cover for the same foxholes. And they seemed to have left in a hurry, leaving one SKS carbine, an M-1 carbine, and a stack of ammunition behind. The two men marveled that they had come so close once again. And that was the way of its ending.

A relatively small affair this one, though a beautifully successful one, it was to have a large consequence.

Baptismal————————
————————and Ambush

For Charley Company (Second Battalion, 8th Infantry), it was a first leap into enemy country, done without benefit of parachutes.

Something went wrong with the chopper pilots. Either they were as green about fighting operations as the infantrymen riding their Hueys or at the last minute their imaginations tricked them and their nerves failed.

While still hovering 10 to 15 feet above the cane brake where they might have set down without too much jar, the pilots said, "Jump!" And the troops, most of them not knowing things weren't done this way, jumped.

Weeks later, after ordeal by fire, they were still bitching about it, not without cause. One machine gunner, Pfc. Thomas Lawlor, leaping into the cane at Plei Yabo, landed on a stump, one ragged edge of which pointed upward like a sharpened spear. The wood tore out the calf of his leg. Other soldiers limped out of the cane to the nearby high ground, where they were to hold briefly, with sprained ankles, torn knees, and multiple bruises.

Bravo Company of the same battalion was to arrive at the cane brake within one hour. They set about clearing

28

the landing zone so that there could be no excuse for the companion outfit's getting the same treatment.

The unauspicious start was on 23 October, 1966, at 1100 hours of a beautifully sunlit day. They had mounted up at Oasis, the extreme western main base regulating operations along the Cambodian border. The troops had been told that there were two NVA regiments in movement through the countryside where they were going, and that was about all that they knew of the mission. There was little other solid information to give them that would have been meaningful.

The two companies spent the next four days moving westward without incident. In that time, they covered not more than 5,000 meters, because it was heavy going all the way, through rock-strewn, bush-covered country, where hill followed hill, with few flat spaces in between, a region riven with numerous rock-walled ravines.

Going west, these two columns marched parallel, about 3,000 meters apart, scouting to the flanks as they moved. It was energy spent without a glimmer of reward. The land appeared to be untenanted. They saw not one person or human habitation and found not a sign that the enemy had ever been there.

The temperature during the marching hours was in the mid-90's, which made the stress doubly acute because they had set forth extremely heavy laden. Each rifleman carried 500 rounds for his M-16, four fragmentation grenades, one smoke grenade, a machete, entrenching tool, two canteens, and three days' rations. The M-79 grenadiers toted 35 rounds apiece. The crews of the M-60 machine guns carried 1,800 rounds. Every other man packed a claymore mine, and two antitank LAW missiles went with each fire team.

"It's enough," commented S.Sgt. James R. Graham,

"to break an old regular's back." Graham, a 36-year-old Texan, was speaking about himself. Bravo Company, counted 132 draftees out of 180 men. Charley, with 140 men, had 111 who had come the same route.

Still, by the end of four days of fruitless slogging along, the men were less worn down than plain bored by what seemed a wild goose chase. That night came news that "jolted them out of their dope." Another outfit from the Fourth Infantry Division had been "hard hit" while in position 7,000 meters to their north and 3,000 meters to the east, which meant to their rear, farther away from Cambodia. They were now to move east in an attempt to close the escape route. The "hard hit" part of it was hyperbole compounded. Weindel's outfit had come through bright-eyed and bushy-tailed.

At first, Charley Company held in place while Bravo Company reconnoitered to the eastward on the following morning, moving four kilometers along the banks of the Se San River. Bravo started in that direction, got new orders, and probed westward for a mile or so. By nightfall, both companies were back at their starting points, with nothing to show for their pains. They had seen no signs, heard no suspicious sounds.

Bravo Company broke camp at first light next morning—0600 on 29 September. It marched in a wedge formation, two platoons in a center column, the other platoons moving along about 100 meters on both sides of the main column and also in single file, one point squad about 50 meters forward of the whole. The front platoon was commanded by Lt. James D. Hunter, 24, of Arlington, Va., regarded by all who knew him as a top-grade soldier. This time they started west. Charley Company got away a few minutes later, moving parallel, not too far away, but over rougher country.

It was a day too fair, for it was boiling hot. The going was dry enough, and the streams so numerous that the canteens did not run low. Still, each column halted briefly 10 times or so to replenish its water supply. By noon, when they broke out rations, both companies were ready to give the war back to Uncle Ho. They almost doubted that Charlie existed. They had searched, prowled, and probed for six more hours and not seen hide nor hair of any human, much less an obvious enemy.

By 1230 they were on the march again, and all the early morning keenness was gone. Worse, they were noisier than before, because the countryside was cor-rugated like a washboard with deep gullies and the men were griping.

As 1300 hours came, there was a startling change; quite suddenly there were signs all about them. Sergeant Graham tripped as he half slid down the sharp bank of a narrow gulch and he went flat "cussing hard." Turning back to see what had thrown him, he found two taut strands of commo wire. He followed the wire to the right along the gulch for about 30 meters where the strands turned with the bank, and there he found a main trail that crossed the gully.

Second Platoon was beating out the ground on that flank and had already found the trail and was following it along. The path was about three feet wide and well beaten. Almost simultaneously, First Platoon entered on it from another angle. Spec. 4 Louis C. Gelada, 22, of Waterbury, Conn., called attention to a rope made of twisted vines attached to the bush on one side; it ran along the trail about hand-high and could be used as a night guide rail. One squad was detailed to check out the trail. S.Sgt. Charles E. Britt, who led it, called attention to sandal tracks: "They're as plain as can be; the dust still holds on the edges. These prints were made minutes ago."

Private First Class Paul D. Mapes, 21, from New Port Richey, Fla., was on ahead, serving as point man. He found three recesses on small embankments next to the trail where food caches had been, and he noted peeled places on some of the trees with Vietnamese characters written on the wood. As he puzzled over these things, he heard several shots fired on ahead and wisely decided he had better turn back.

What had happened was that one fire team from the platoon's Second Squad, not getting the word, had blundered into the trail at a point on beyond Mapes. Where they entered, the trail ran straight. Standing in clear view, 100 meters uptrail, were two khaki-clad figures. The men snap-fired, and they missed. The quarry scuttled away. At that point, the entire platoon was called back and the squads were dressed in line to sweep the area. Nothing important came of it.

Specialist 4 Don Williams, 21, of Houston, an RTO (radio telephone operator), was carrying the battalion radio. When Second Platoon found the commo wire, Capt. John A. Noble and others in the Charley Company CP group moved up to it. As they arrived, an air strike was laid on about 2,000 meters to the west of where they stood. This was designed to soften up the area where Bravo Company would spend the night, and it was nothing more than a precaution. Noble had already tapped the enemy wire. (This is done by putting the TA-1 telephone set on it, after stripping the insulation.) As each bomb fell, they heard Vietnamese voices jabbering in high excitement over the wire. For lack of an interpreter, they did not know what was being said. Still, common sense told them that they were in the immediate presence of an enemy force, though they didn't know exactly where it was.

Noble had heard enough. It was time for his company to pull up and go into perimeter. Later, calling on the guns, he would work over the ground round about with 105-mm. fire.

The trail ran almost due west toward Cambodia, and Bravo Company had to go that way. The skipper, Capt. Alfred D. Jones, a Philadelphian, said to Lieutenant Hunter, "Move on west, clearing trail as you go, and report to me."

The platoon slogged along single file, every man on the trail, and its noise discipline must have suddenly become nigh perfect. It was the beginning of their schooling in special caution. Toward the end of the journey the path veered sharply and started uphill. Sgt. Bobbie Hill, a Tennesseean, was the point man.

As Hill made the turn, there sat a khaki-clad figure on a tree stump, his face turned the other way, his rifle slung over his shoulder. Hill was viewing an enemy in the field for the first time—and it threw him. At five-feet range, he fired his M-16 rifle once—and missed. The North Vietnamese slid away into the bush. What Hill said is unprintable.

A moment later came a blast from the other direction. Spec. 4 Claude Green was bringing up the rear of the column, armed with a shotgun. When Hill fired, Green faced about. Fifteen feet away, in clear view on the trail, stood another North Vietnamese. Green fired one round —missed—and the target vanished. These sounds front and rear, more than the failures, shook the platoon to the marrow.

Hunter reported the incidents back to Captain Jones on the RT and was told: "Get into perimeter as quickly as possible." This happened about 1400.

Hunter considered. The top of the hill mass on their
right was the designated ground. But because there
seemed to be many Charlies around and the trail took
another dip amid heavy brush where it veered toward
the high ground, he thought he had best deploy the platoon to make a brief recon of the low ground before
tackling the hill.

So he split the platoon. Sgt. David Brown of Olive
Hill, Ky., was sent to the left with his fire team to search
one branch of the main trail. Hunter led the main body
to the right along the main trail. He had changed his
point man. It was now Sgt. Andis Hill.

One hundred meters beyond and 15 minutes after the
last incident, Andis Hill suddenly froze and motioned
with his hand to Hunter to come up. Hunter joined him
and his eyes bugged: coming along the trail toward him,
not more than 80 meters away, were five North Vietnamese, chattering away at a great rate, obviously inap-
prehensive, their rifles slung.

Hunter's group set up their ambush in the next 10
seconds, by the end of which time the targets were 15 or
so meters closer. The Viets kept coming. As they closed
to within 25 meters, Plat. Sgt. David L. Keller of
Hagerstown, Md., whispered, "Now!" Keller opened
fire with his M-16. Pfc. Leonard Cario of New York
City was at the M-60 machine gun, with Pfc. Billy Doss
of Los Angeles helping him. They opened fire but the
bullet stream was about 10 meters high. Hunter was
working his M-16 as fast as he could; he spent one whole
magazine.

The result was zero. The North Vietnamese disappeared uptrail at a run. At the spot where the enemy
group had come under fire, Hunter's men found two
small blood trails, a few minor pieces of equipment that
had been shot loose, and a cap, but no rifles.

Hunter was not disconsolate: he was sore as hell. "We're the lousiest damned shots I've heard of in my life," he said to the others.

The men continued to move on toward the hill. But they moved very slowly. There was much more commo wire along the trail but it didn't interest them at all. They knew blue funk.

The other platoons were in motion, proceeding methodically along the trail. In the distance, they heard the sounds of the shooting, greatly muffled by two intervening hills. To the ears of Plat. Sgt. Charles W. Turner it sounded like a "sure-as-hell" fight and, when it suddenly stopped, he said, "Sounds as if we made a big score."

Platoon Sergeant James T. Douglas of the Third arrived first at the base of the hill with an advance party. He had been given the special mission of reconnoitering, and, if necessary, clearing the designated landing zone for receiving supplies.

What he saw dismayed him. The spot was on low ground, thorny, and fixed with rock slabs badly tilted and too large to move. "I'm going to change this in a hurry," he said. Douglas split the squad in two to search for a better LZ. What they found was a suitably flat rectangle of ground 300 meters up one of the ridge fingers and 150 yards off the main trail.

Hunter had already sent out three patrols to comb the ridge slopes for enemy signs, though with negative results. The other men had immediately begun preparing the position and Hunter noted that they dug feverishly, going deeper than was their habit. One of the diggers told him, "We know something is going to happen tonight." By the time the main body approached the base of the hill (about 1700 hours, less than an hour before dark), the position was already out of the water. Water-

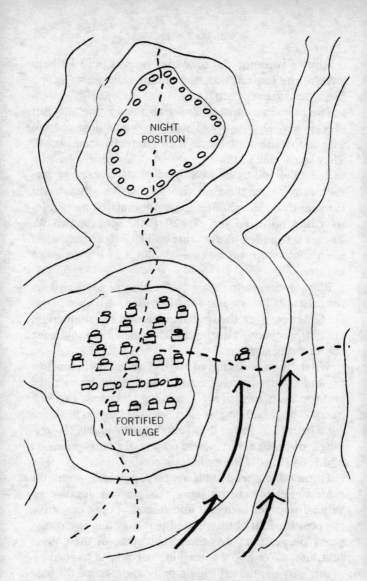

Arrows indicate Charley's Company advance toward fortified village. After light contact, troops went into a defensive perimeter for the night above village.

carrying parties were sent to the creek 300 or so meters from the hill base to take care of that problem.

As the column arrived at the foot of the hill, Hunter joined the van to lead the way up and to give the men around him a quick rundown on what had happened. The lieutenant was wearing an enemy cap, and part of his audience was not exactly friendly. Striding along with him at the front of Third Platoon was its leader, Plat. Sgt. James A. Moore, a 30-year-old Negro from Waynesville, N.C., 11 years in the Regular Army.

"I ain't got a bit of sympathy," said Moore. "With all that fire power, how could you miss five Charlies?"

Hunter simply shook his head. "You tell me," he said.

There was much work to do within and around the perimeter. Tall stands of bamboo and thick brush choked off the fields of fire and limited the view within the foxhole line. So they fell to with machetes and were still hacking away when daylight died. It was 1800 hours straight up when they heard for the first time that Charley Company had been engaged, or rather was kept tilting with a puzzling problem, for several hours. Battalion communications were not working to the best advantage that day.

The keen eyes of the pilot of a "Bird Dog" aircraft —a light plane with fixed wings—had pulled Captain Noble and his company from their defensive perimeter shortly before mid-afternoon. "I see a fortified village about 600 meters directly to the northwest of you," the airman messaged, "and I see people moving around in it." The company had heard no sounds from that direction.

Noble drew his lieutenants and sergeants close together and told them how to form for the attack—Second Platoon in line on the left, Third Platoon in the center, and First on the right, with the CP group trailing the center by about 40 meters. A deep ravine, which 2nd Lt. Benjamin F. Maxham's Third Platoon in the center had to straddle, clove the flat all the way to the rim of the village, which sat on a slight rise. They started at 1300. Advancing, Maxham's men, 200 meters along, missed one skirmisher hiding behind a bush at the bottom of the ravine. The Charlie fired at Noble, but the shooting was wild. Pfc. Richard Bridges returned fire, but he also missed. This was the company's baptism—a mild one, at that. So they held in place briefly to check out the immediate vicinity, and, after finding nothing, moved on another 100 meters as planned.

Then came a call from Second Platoon's leader, 2nd Lt. Elwood R. Tauscher, a New Yorker: "We've moved up to a hut, with two heavy-walled bunkers at either end. Shall I destroy it?"

"Go ahead," Noble answered.

Tauscher's men exploded two grenades in each of the bunkers without really hurting them.

Lieutenant James R. Helberg, USMA '65, who led the First Platoon, called in, "We can hear a lot of voices to our left front, mixed voices, men and women. Sounds like they're coming from the ravine. Should be directly to Maxham's front. Shall I hold the position?"

"Hold where you are for 15 minutes," Noble said.

By the end of that time the voices had faded out altogether, so Noble told all platoons, "Move on."

Two minutes later Helberg reported over the RT, "I have the whole village in sight."

It was then 1445.

"Second will move to the left of the village and secure," Noble ordered. "First will swing around to the right of it, but not enter." So First Platoon closed.

Private Mapes, being with First Squad, First Platoon,

was flank security for the whole, the one man closest to the huts. What he heard completely baffled him—women screaming, men shouting and beating on sticks, but still holding their ground. The company had done no firing; nothing had threatened the village from above. Noble had deliberately held his line back so that civilians would not be killed by mistake. Helberg was no less puzzled by the commotion and how to respond. Lest things get out of hand, he withdrew his men to the ravine. He suspected an attack might be launched.

Second Platoon, which had to skirt a bend in the ravine, got to the village a few minutes later. The place was now vacated; its tumultuous inhabitants had withdrawn to the rear. Left behind were one enfeebled Montagnard woman with an ancient face, withered as a dried apple, quite a few pigs, and many chickens. Search of the more than 30 hootches, begun at once, continued for an hour. The loot, piled high in the center of the village, included three boxes of ammunition, eight bags of rice, ten khaki uniforms, one Chinese overcoat, and a Russian pistol. A case-hard fighting bunker was found next to every dwelling. Noble looked these things over, then said, "Start killing the pigs." (He meant the porkers.) He knew at last, and a little too late, that he was dealing with an enemy community.

At 1500 Noble gave the order to First and Second Platoons: "Move on out and start preparing our position for night defense." He had already decided that the village had to be destroyed. Though the huts were markedly new, there was already camouflage over the top of each and the foliage was being shaped to hide them completely. The departure of the platoon column left Third Platoon, Weapons Platoon, and the Command Post group to take care of the village.

Sergeant Graham took care of the demolitions.

Satchel charges were detonated in every bunker; Graham noted that each bunker was so placed as to support two other bunkers. Third Platoon was then about to wrap up the operation by burning the houses, placing a basket of burning faggots in each.

Private First Class Kenneth L. Maddy, a good-natured 19-year-old from Utah, was doing outguard duty on the village fringe. He thought he saw movement along the trail, dropped to his knees, and said to the others, "I see a gink. He's in khaki." Then he shifted a little forward and to the right for a better view, to make certain; Lieutenant Maxham was directly to his left. From downtrail, an AK-47 rifle opened fire on Maddy and the burst drilled his body just to the right of the navel. He was dead within 15 minutes.

These are characteristic acts, doubts, and hesitations by an Army that has been accused by clergymen, including the late Rev. Dr. Martin Luther King Jr., of going about carelessly slaughtering innocents at the rate of hundreds of thousands a year. Senator Edward M. Kennedy of Massachusetts has aired the same hurtful charge, relying on slanted or falsified statistics.

Graham jumped downtrail 10 feet in front of Maddy firing his M-16 rifle on full automatic as he lunged. It was too late. Graham returned to Maddy. "I'm hit," the kid said. "I'm hit. I'm sorry." He died while the sergeant lay there, trying to comfort him. As Graham reloaded, he had called "No. 10!" very loudly, and the platoon medic, Pfc. James Abraham, had come on the double. So had Pfc. Hunter A. Manney, the aid man of the other platoon. They had knelt with Graham and Maxham and one of them had cried a bit, because clearly bandages would do no good.

It was the first death in the company. How would a hard-boiled NCO, many years in the Regular Army, born and reared west of Fort Worth, which is cow country, react to it? Graham stood and emptied two more magazines from his M-16, firing downtrail—a completely silly gesture, a waste of ammunition, in a venting of what gets deep inside a man in his darkest moments. Graham had to do it, and he did it. Maybe he blamed himself a little, but there was no good reason for it.

Vincent Arceo, 34, of Guam, a first sergeant with 15 years in the Regular Army, had stayed with Noble in the center of the village and heard the call for "No. 10!" He had sent the company aid man, Spec. 4 Dave L. Barber, on the run. Seldom has one fighter in death been so well attended. Barber returned and told Arceo and Noble, "He's dead." They didn't talk about it; there was no point. Arceo, a short, stocky soldier with a normally jovial nature, sat silent.

Noble suddenly made up his mind. "We'll have to call back the other two platoons," the captain said. His reasoning was elementary. The din raised by the Montagnards had not been spontaneous but contrived; it had sounded too strident to be other than a signal, either to warn or to alert an unseen force of NVA. But what was the purpose beyond that? Suppose that the villagers, having raised their clatter, had then hastily pulled out so that they would be pursued. The object would be to lure the company into an already fixed ambush. Better than risk bumping such a force while moving to the two other platoons, Noble would make camp around the village.

But Lieutenant Tauscher, on returning with Second Platoon, talked the captain out of his plan: "There's a knoll just a couple of hundred meters west of the village that looks excellent for night defense," Tauscher said.

Lieutenant Colonel Lounsbury, the battalion CO (commanding officer), who was overhead in his Huey at the moment, scouted the knoll and approved the arrangement. The two footloose platoons moved onto the knoll at once; the other elements completed the destruction of the village. And there was more done than that. The main trail that ran through the village also cut directly across the cap of the knoll. They reckoned that, if an attack came, it would strike from the direction of the village. So an engineer squad that had been detailed to the company was ordered to clear a 10-foot-wide path around the village, which required the blowing up of 17 large trees. The knoll was also forest-crowned; logs hewed from inside the perimeter were used to revet its face, outside the foxhole line.

It was dusk when the work was finished, and Weapons Platoon, along with Third, settled into that half of the night position that was nearest the village, their outpost line within grenade-throwing range of the village edge. An air drop came in as the platoons closed. The bundles were loaded with C-rations, explosives, and mail. Nothing dropped wrong but the mail. Noble ordered the C-rations withheld until the late-arriving platoons had finished their digging. "Get those foxholes deep enough and you'll feel hungrier," he said. The forward observer, 2nd Lt. James Bragg (A/4/42nd), regulated the dropping of defensive fires four ways from the perimeter as dark fell, to the wasting of whatever ammunition was used. Then the three-man outposts in front of each platoon were pulled back to the circle, and four-man listening posts were established, 30 meters outside the foxhole line. So placed, they were much too close to be of any real benefit.

The meal over, Noble called his officers together, quickly briefed them on the developments leading to his decision, and then gave his estimate: "We'll have a full moon in a few minutes. They know we're expecting them, so they won't come early. They'll wait till the camp's asleep. I expect it after midnight. And I want you to get some sleep now. You'll need it."

It was sound reasoning throughout. The lieutenants bought it, returned to their platoons to do a little cheer-leading, then all settled in their foxholes except Maxham, who flattened in the open and was asleep by 2230. He was awakened at 0230 by small arms-fire, and with one bound he was in his foxhole. Though the opening probe came against his sector only, men of the company were working their weapons all around the perimeter.

Of the four men in the listening post of Maxham's platoon, the two that were charged with staying alert had drowsed off. All might have been overrun and killed but for the fact that Pfc. Robert Baker and Pfc. George Radford, who had stood the last watch, were about half-awake. Under a bright moon, they saw the Charlies—five of them—directly to their front, for the first time, when they were not more than 10 meters off. The enemy came at a walk, rifles slung over their shoulders.

Radford whispered, "Remain silent."

"No, we gotta fire," Baker said.

He pulled the trigger, but got off only two rounds. The weapon jammed.

From behind the Vietnamese skirmishers half a dozen AK-47's poured fire right at the two men, and a grenade sailed in, exploding next to the listening post.

The volley was terribly accurate. Radford, Pfc. David Villanueva, and Pfc. Lewis Dake were all hit by bullets and grenade frags, and the wounds were deep.

Within three minutes, Dake and Baker had crawled back to Maxham. "Villanueva and Rad are sitting out there wounded," Baker reported. "I don't think they can move. But the LP has not been overrun. They're still fighting."

By this time machine-gun and rifle fire had enveloped Third Platoon's sector throughout and was also engaging part of Weapons Platoon, though, except for the group that had flattened against the LP, the enemy seemed loath to come out of the woods and tighten the pressure. Two of First Platoon's foxholes also drew fire; men from Weapons Platoon swung over to reenforce Maxham's line. The hot exchange lasted not more than five minutes. Before it tapered off, Villanueva came crawling back.

From the foxhole near Maxham, a machine gunner, Pfc. Robert P. Reed, cried out, "I see one! I see one!" He picked up the gun in his arms and went into a crouch, as if waiting for a clearer view. A bullet hit him in the shoulder and spun him around. One of his mates shouted, "No. 10! No. 10!"

Private Manney, sitting next to Maxham, said cheerfully, "That's my number. Guess I gotta go."

Maxham grabbed him by the seat of the pants. "You wait here till the fire stops," the lieutenant, using his head, said.

In that second the attack stopped as the enemy broke contact and drew off. Pfc. Arch Moseley had quickly taken over Reed's gun and put it into action. The two guns were several paces in front of the line, so placed that their fires crossed. It was the gun on the right, under the hand of Spec. 4 Fred Dixon, that had wrought most of the execution, though until the lull came the Americans had no idea that they had scored.

Then from the darkness, just outside the perimeter, Arceo could hear the screams and moaning of many wounded. From a greater distance, beyond the tree line, came the shouts of enemy leaders exhorting their men. "I guess we're doing all right," the sergeant said to Captain Noble.

At a still greater distance, Jones, Hunter, and Bravo Company were getting all these developments quite clearly over radio. Hunter had been eavesdropping when the first shots were fired. He made the rounds; the company went on 100 percent alert.

It had surprised Maxham that the Americans had quit shooting as soon as the enemy fire ceased. He had not expected the fire discipline of a green company to be that good. For that, much of the credit must go to Noble, an extraordinary soldier. A Citadel graduate, 26 years old, chosen by the Jaycees as one of the nation's 10 outstanding young men, mayor of his home town in Georgia, Noble was fighting in Vietnam only because when the call came, as a Reservist, he demanded that he be given active duty. He had won the love of Charley Company, and also the professional respect of the veteran NCO's.

The lull lasted only three minutes. In that time Manney treated Reed and Dake. The rush was on again before he could get to Radford.

In the second round, the enemy attacked over a 50-meter front, which left two-thirds of the defensive circle relatively nonengaged. The volume of fire indicated there were two North Vietnamese Army companies assaulting. Noble had collected his M-79 gunners and had them fire in salvo at the first area where he figured the Vietnamese were regrouping, judging by the sounds. It was one of his better tricks.

The enemy came on again, less raggedly than the first time, at least half of the line standing, walking straight ahead, and firing as it advanced. The wonder is that the North Vietnamese tried it the second time. More than half of the 160-meter defensive circle was protected by a deep gorge, the rock walls of which did a bend just beyond the foxhole line. (The position was at YA-

671-516.) This natural strength kept Second Platoon's sector nonengaged, and its members acted as reenforcers and ammo bearers for Maxham's men and the few positions of First Platoon under the bullet hail. Noble did not have to urge them. Tauscher had chosen the position well.

Just before the fight flared again, Lieutenant Bragg, the FO (forward observer), whose spot overlooked the gorge, came running to Noble to ask if he wanted artillery. Noble told him to get busy. It wasn't that easy. Bragg's radio, like the others, was interdicted and could only relay through Bravo Company.

The ground where Third Platoon defended was formidable. In order to break the line, the North Vietnamese had to advance 15 to 20 meters upward over a 30-degree rock-strewn slope, and although the felled timber gave them some cover, it was also an obstacle for the enemy soldiers.

In this situation, the two machine guns off the flanks still bore the main burden. Dixon, after firing 1,200 rounds, handed over to his assistant and ran to Second Platoon's sector to get more ammo. Moseley fired 800 rounds. Noble stood ready with a reserve of two squads from Second Platoon, should the line be breached anywhere. The moon was gone, the sky overcast, the darkness complete. Riflemen fired in any direction from which they heard voices. So did the M-79 gunners. These were the conditions of a repulse that in 15 minutes became total, then final.

Still, it was a win not without tears. Pfc. William G. Mansfield of King's Point, N.Y., an 81-mm. mortarman who had stood to use an M-79 launcher, was wounded by a bullet that hit him in the right temple and came out the left. He died within the hour. S.Sgt. Roger L. Nobotne of Second Squad was drilled by a bullet through the left eye. As the attack subsided, Baker, Manney, and Pfc. Paul A. Johnson ran downslope and carried Radford back to the perimeter. He had been hit in six places and was paralyzed from one frag wound that got him in the spine. Months later, he was still in hospital, unable to walk. Villanueva, after being operated on three times, ultimately returned to the company.

Bragg, after much frustration, made it in the closing minutes. An observer in a Huey had appeared overhead; he became the relay to the guns. At the same time, Noble heard from the battalion S-3, Capt. William Harvey, that "Puff is on his way; come up on the same 'bush' with it." "Bush" was code for "frequency," Puff's frequency, which Harvey passed along. So in a situation where Noble's men had no real chance for pursuit because of the darkness, the artillery and the plane with the big whammy were turned on in time to harass and possibly damage the enemy on his way out.

Proud of his men, aware that they had performed like veterans, Noble, the well-named soldier, still felt miserable. Through the last minutes he had heard over his radio that Bravo Company was taking a pounding, and he reflected bitterly that he was not in position to do anything about it.

Unlike Noble and his men, Jones and Bravo Company had made their camp on unsatisfactory ground with no time left to do anything about it, except prepare partway. Without doubt, they had been followed to the hill, and the enemy had probably observed their every move. The Americans had been pushed hard on the trail, to close with such little daylight as was left them. They had rushed to get water, and their digging and such clearing as they did was under great pressure, though they were already fatigued and hungry. It is questionable whether under these conditions, and in view of the midday incidents that rather clearly indicated they were detected, it was the better part of wisdom to hold to the original plan and split the two companies. The timing of the onfall against the two perimeters suggests that this is exactly what the enemy expected them to do, and that the NVA deployments were arranged accordingly. Each company was tactically on its own. Yet heavy weapons support from outside had not been preset so that there would be immediate help for either. There were no mortars on Bravo's hill; the machine guns were rather casually dug in.

The crown of the hill was outcropped with rim rock and the slopes were strewn with slabs and boulders. The perimeter was about 50 by 100 meters, with variations in elevation running 10 feet or more from foxhole to foxhole due to the crinkling of the ridge top. Good management cannot of itself compensate for bad ground. The fields of fire varied in breadth from 10 to 20 meters. Beyond the limited clearing, the trees and shrubs were densely grown. There was no grass anywhere.

Five-man listening posts had been put downslope about 25 meters to the front of each platoon one hour after dark came, the company having labored to whip the position into shape until that time. Everybody felt uneasy and there was little sleeping up to the moment when Noble's men got hit, except for men who were so dog-tired that, drooping a little, they dropped off.

As with the attack on the other hill, the fight began with a limited assault against the LP's, and because of the sharpness of the slope, they fought in isolation, with the main body getting little feeling about what was going on and having no chance to help effectively.

Lieutenant Hunter, on radio, had heard the opening rounds go off when Private Baker started Charley Company's fight. He passed the word along to, among others, Platoon Sergeant Turner, leader of Bravo's Weapons Platoon. Turner, who comes from Anniston, Ala., was the oldest man present, with 22 of his 46 years spent in the Regular Army. This was his third war. Turner was allowed not more than one minute to chew over what Hunter had reported; then he heard explosions to his front, down the slope, and he guessed that the platoon's listening post was making the racket.

The LP had not been caught unawares, though Pvt. Joseph Key, the man detailed to watch, was dozing slightly. Fully awake, mainly because he "didn't feel right about things," was Pfc. Harold Steele of Cincinnati, who had not gone beyond tenth grade in public school, but was no dropout in battle. Steele knew that he was on listening-post duty, and, though it was his first time, he had already reckoned that this meant listening hard. An original character this one, with no real feeling for learning, but possessed of a remarkable ability to soak up knowledge quickly because of an acute interest in the nature of things, plus applied common sense. He had the right moment for his talents.

Steele heard the tree branches crackling and a rustling in the bush. He tapped Key on the shoulder and said, "Hey, that's not the wind." Their eyes strained forward, and Steele saw three North Vietnamese standing about 20 feet away, so close that the sight of their webbed gear and slung rifles stayed memorable. They "gawked" at Steele as if surprised to see him. His M-16 was beside him, but unfortunately Key had it pinned under one knee. Steele lunged for it. As their bodies came together, Pfc. Jose Valcarcel, a Puerto Rican, shot the leading Charlie in the head. Then all three Americans fired. A fourth Vietnamese, whom Steele had not seen at all, opened fire with an AK-47. The other two Viets ran left, as if to get on the rear of the

LP. The AK-47 fire was very high, very wild. Valcarcel turned to deal with the other two men. The listening post was spread around a little knob. From out of darkness a potato-masher grenade landed, exploding on the top of the knob, but nobody got hurt. Steele propped on his elbows to look for the thrower. Another grenade sailed in, hit Steele on the right elbow, struck a nerve, and paralyzed the arm, then bounced off and dudded. A third grenade missed completely. The enemy grenadier thought he had wiped out the LP. Leaving his tree stump, he emerged in the open. Luckily, Steele is a southpaw. He stood, heaved his grenade at the target, and the explosion almost decapitated the Charlie, so perfect were the toss and the timing. They had carried on this small bout in utter silence after the first warning. Now Steele said, "Everybody back to the perimeter!" He went straight to Jones. "Captain," he said, "I want to tell you what happened." Jones was prepared to listen, but they were interrupted.

The company's executive officer, Lt. Richard Larsen, was getting a report from another listening post. It was Pfc. Daniel Nolff on the radio. "I'm hearing something," Nolff said. "It sounds like bushes crackling as if bodies were coming through."

"Everybody's hearing things tonight," Larsen answered. "You stay where you are. Wait until you verify." Nolff was back on the radio in two minutes. "I can see them now," he said. "They're 15 meters away."

"If you can stay there without being seen, don't fire," Larsen ordered.

A few seconds passed, then came a frantic call from Nolff: "They're on me! I'm going to fire."

"Then use grenades," Larsen shouted.

Nolff went off the radio. The listeners heard explosions and screams from down the slope. There were also yells from Vietnamese throats as the general attack came on.

One would wish it were possible to draw the veil on this small incident. Nolff, a 20-year-old from South Broadman, Mich, had been badly wounded in the side, and he died the following morning. Sgt. John Babiak of Newark dragged himself back to the perimeter from the listening post, his left leg smashed by a bullet, the bone sticking from the flesh. Pvt. Joe Vance, a Californian who had just come to the company, got partway up the slope, then collapsed; his left foot and leg had been mangled by a grenade. Under fire, Turner and several others went forth and brought him in. Vance said, "Nolff is out there somewhere—I don't know just where." Turner started out to get him. That was when the Vietnamese rifle line swarmed forward and enemy mortars ranged in atop the hill. Turner had to turn back; so Nolff was left, forsaken but not forgotten, until morning. It should not have happened.

Other ironies were to follow immediately, along with much iron. What happened to each man for good and bad in those heart-stopping, high-low moments of their first combat would be a story in itself. There is room for only a few, some of them reminiscent of Siegfried Sassoon's haunting phrase, "this world of blundering warfare." Joel Fosdick (inevitably nicknamed "Fearless"), a second lieutenant who was the forward artillery observer, had done himself proud. Having his wind up because of the earlier contacts along the trail, he had made certain that the 105's of Bravo Battery (4/42nd) would be on tap, and the gunners rabbit-eared for his call. But the hasty preparation of the position had blocked any chance to register fires. Game to the core, Fosdick at once told the battery to fire away.

A first round hit and destroyed the M-60 machine gun

of the engineer squad fighting with the company. One shard hit Pfc. Tim Cullen in the chest and cut through his dogtag chain before lodging in his flesh. The tags fell to earth through one flapping pants leg, and he could not find them. Ignoring his wound, Cullen moved about crying, "I've lost my dogtags. Help me find them." At the moment, this struck no one as ludicrous. The tags were found in a crack in the rocks the next morning.

This was nothing compared to the way the boom was lowered on Platoon Sergeant Moore, who had razzed Lieutenant Hunter in late afternoon. Second Platoon's sector, under 2nd Lt. Americus Gill, USMA '65, was unengaged as the fight began; its listening post went undisturbed and promptly withdrew to the perimeter. All hands held their fire, not sweating because they were denied a piece of the action, but for the moment feeling lucky.

Gill passed the order to move one machine gun over to help Weapons Platoon. Moore stood in his foxhole to shout the word to Sgt. Virgil B. Hardy. Just then a cluster of mortar shells exploded into the platoon position. They kept coming. Within the next five minutes somewhere between 40 and 50 rounds of 82-mm. mortar rocked this one sector, the main position hit, the only heavy stuff fired by the enemy during the night.

The first salvo lifted Moore out of his foxhole and blew him 20 feet down the slope. One shard had cut through his steel pot and lodged in his head. He came to rest still conscious, but badly stunned.

He knew he was wounded somewhere in the head, but not much more. He was temporarily stone deaf to all but one sound. So he told himself that the wound must be in his ear. The illusion grew that a grenade was planted inside his head. He could hear the grenade ticking away, and he wondered dully when it would go off.

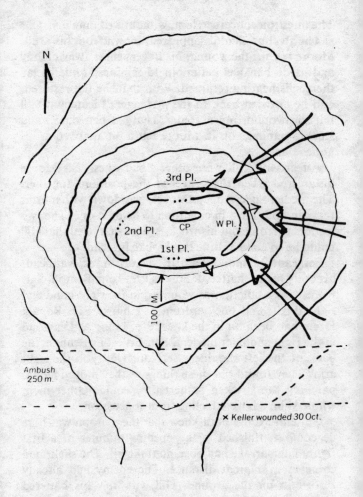

The hill where Bravo Company was mortared. Large arrows indicate enemy attacks against platoon positions, small arrows U.S. counterfire. Ambush is to west.

The question concerned him, without agitating him.

The steel pot had disappeared, blown from his skull. Moore felt for the wound; his fingers came away bloody and made him feel better. In 15 minutes, while he lay there, his hearing returned. With that, he felt restored, and he crawled back to the perimeter. Lieutenant Gill felt the wound, murmured, "That's a bad one," and stuck a bandage on it. Moore felt a bit annoyed at his nonchalance.

All around Gill were other "bad ones," as Moore discovered when they checked the positions together. The medic, Spec. 4 Jack Dankel, was down with mortar frags in both hips, in condition to help no one. The two leaders perforce did his work. Moore marveled that Gill could be so good at little things, like first aid.

Sergeant Raymond Pearl Jr., a Korean vet, was dead, his body badly shattered. So was Pfc. John Benton. Sgt. Robert W. Mallette was wounded in the right hand and right thigh, and one eardrum had burst. Pfc. Ronald Firem had been hit in the knee, Pfc. Louis A. Diamond in the right shoulder blade, S.Sgt. Ernest L. Behm in the back of the left shoulder, Sergeant Hardy in the right arm. They found out these things as they moved along, patching the stricken as best they could. Other men, whole-skinned, were reeling from concussion.

Gill and Moore both knew that the platoon was hors de combat, finished in the opening minutes of a first fight. The barrage had been no fluke hit. The shells had come in over great distance. The enemy had already zeroed in on the ground. Gill withdrew his battered people to the CP, where they waited.

On the heels of the mortaring, the enemy rifle attack was pressed over a narrow front, avoiding where the shelling had opened a gaping hole and hitting instead against the sectors of First and Weapons Platoons and the engineer squad. The spread was not more than 50 meters. Even there, the advance was ragged and uncertain. Most of the Vietnamese halted at the edge of the wood line; not more than a dozen came forward into the open where they could be seen. They fired, but they walked like drunken men, and they screamed at the tops of their voices. A still wilder screaming, with the pitch of many more voices, came from out of the trees. It curdled Hunter's blood. He turned to Turner, saying, "I think they're doped." Turner agreed. "It sounds like it."

The M-79 grenadiers concentrated their fire against the wood line. Pvt. James D. Caron, Seattle; Pfc. Richard B. Winton, New York City, and Pfc. Patrick A. Francis, Boston, shared a common foxhole. These were the stalwarts who, with one M-60 machine gun, several M-16 rifles, and a few grenades, wiped out the pack that drove toward the perimeter. This was done at 10-meter range. Another enemy group of five men, two of them firing machine guns as they marched, was cut down in front of Weapons Platoon.

So there was a first swift repulse following a tempest that, seeming too long, lasted not more than four minutes. Hunter, his mind concentrated on the rifle assault, did not know till then that he had lost six men WIA (wounded in action) and one KIA (killed in action) to the mortar barrage. Pfc. Carroll D. Abbott, a Nashville boy, was dead. The worst wounded were the platoon aid man, Pfc. Gary Hughes, disabled by a shard in his right hand, and Pfc. Glenn Draughn, a Floridian, whose right shoulder was shattered by the same burst that got Abbott.

Private First Class Harry Evans was also hit in the shoulder. A big hunk of steel went through the stock of an M-16 carried by Sgt. James Baldree with such force that it broke his right arm. Pfc. Billy Doss, a First Platoon machine gunner, took a mortar frag in his back, but stayed on the gun all night. Pfc. Jules Cario had his left Achilles tendon cut through, and Pfc. Ira Graham was wounded in the back.

There were losses elsewhere in the company from this same dreadful shelling. Act. Sgt. Raymond Doss, 21, of Harlan, Ky., had his stomach torn open; he died during the night. A Baltimore boy, Act. Sgt. Richard L. Chase, was temporarily paralyzed by a shard lodged near the base of his spine.

So it was mortar, mortar, mortar trouble for the only two aid men in condition to work, 21-year-old Spec. Salvador Decerra of Banning, Calif., and Pfc. Billy G. Winter of Minneapolis. Said Decerra to Winter, "Good this isn't a real big fight."

A 20-minute lull followed the enemy recoil. Hunter noted that the Vietnamese withdrew to the base of the hill, though they would have been in defilade a few meters beyond the tree line. The screaming and shrieking continued from the distance. "I guess they're getting another shot in the arm," Hunter remarked.

When the Vietnamese came on the second time, he felt certain he was right about it. There was no more mortaring; the battery must have fired everything it had. The riflemen came staggering up the slope as uncertainly as the first time, and in about the same numbers. When firing, the enemy rifles were held at various angles, and the aim was very erratic.

That was not the silly part of it. As they closed to within easy killing distance, one of the Charlies in front yelled out, "Hey, GI, tell me what time it is?"

"Who the f—— wants to know?" an American voiced answer.

So the enemy soldier tried again: "Hey, GI, you don't belong in Vietnam."

From out of Weapons Platoon someone roared back, "Well, Buddy, we sure as hell are here."

So ended the conversation. Here was no ordinary malignant determination: the execution was too grotesque. Bored with the talk, the foxhole line opened fire and another swath of Vietnamese was washed out of the war. There were no more charges or even a trancelike facsimile of one. Small-arms and machine-gun fire continued to keep the Americans close to cover until 0450, all of it coming from beyond the tree line and none of it doing real damage. Five or six men were nicked by bullets glancing off rocks; none was hurt seriously. The final checkout showed that two more men out of Third Platoon had been hit by mortar frags in the deadly three minutes when the curtain went up. Pfc. Stacey D. Swingle had a deep flesh wound in his right hip and Pfc. Gene F. Schutt had a shard in his left calf. They had kept mum about it.

Puff the Magic Dragon came flying on from the other hill. The minigun fire intended for the Vietnamese beyond the tree line almost browned out the friendly foxholes. Distressed by the erratic fire, Turner built a blaze out of ponchos and mosquito nets to show the pilot where the defending line ran, after which the minigun did a little better—not much, but some.

A steady drizzle set in as the shooting tapered off. With dawn came the onerous task of policing the battlefield. The men counted 47 bodies strewn over the slopes, which was all they ever claimed, though they estimated they had killed at least 200. Also, they collected 26 weapons—AK-47 rifles, and three machine guns. Later they learned it had been an NVA battalion in the attack, the First of the 33rd Regiment. The only remarkable thing about the next hour or so was the nigh unbroken silence. They worked, but no one felt like talking.

At 0800 Captain Jones came to Hunter and said, "I want some of your people to run a sweep down the ridge forward of your lines." That was the way the trail ran. Hunter called for volunteers. They were eager enough. Sergeant Keller took charge of the patrol. Sergeant Brown went along as his second. With them were Pfc. Daniel "Flash" Phillips, Olive Hill, Ky.; Pfc. Richard Musto, Brooklyn, and Pfc. Martin Barretto, Los Angeles. Keller carried a few grenades. The others had only M-16 rifles. They took off with a rush, fairly bouncing along. The enemy had fled; no one was thinking of ambushes.

Ten minutes passed. Then, from downtrail, Hunter heard the sounds of heavy firing. Brown's voice came to him pitched above the sounds of fire: "Aid man! Aid man! Bring ammunition." Stuffing a dozen M-16 magazines in his shirt, Hunter dashed for them, running as fast as the trail permitted.

Halfway down the ridge (about 125 meters) Hunter came upon the scene. Keller was down, hit three times by bullets in the right arm, chest, and back. Keller had seen three khaki-clad figures ahead on the trail with their backs turned; as he went for a grenade, a burst of automatic fire toppled him before he could pull the pin. Barretto had already killed the man who had downed Keller, but the burst got him in the chest. Brown had shot one sniper out of a tree and killed a third man as he ran from a bamboo thicket.

In the second or two that Hunter took it all in, an enemy machine gun opened fire on him 20 meters from where Keller lay. Hunter, zigzagging, tossed the extra magazines to the flattened members of the patrol as he passed, still running for the enemy gun. He was firing the M-16 without aiming as he went. Fifteen yards beyond where Keller lay, his own rifle jammed. (Hunter, a graduate mechanical engineer from Georgia Tech, despised this weapon.) A dozen or so enemy bullets fanned his legs, several cutting the cloth of his fatigues without breaking skin. By rare luck, just then the NVA gunner finished his drum and the weapon went silent.

Hunter knelt to throw a grenade. He was still trying to strip the tape from the bomb when the machine gun resumed fire, now at 30-meter range. The lieutenant threw the grenade, charged on a few feet, and literally stumbled across an abandoned enemy light machine gun—the RPD. He pulled the trigger; the RPD worked perfectly. Hunter got off 50 or so rounds against the enemy gunner. That position went silent. Then a second machine gun opened fire on Hunter, this time from directly to his left. Hunter fired another 50 rounds that way; the gun quit.

Suddenly everything was silent, except that Keller was screaming high in pain. "Don't touch me!" he yelled. "Don't touch me!" Backing off, Hunter had to bully and curse his men to get them to lift Keller. Then they got with it, the others trying to walk Keller along, supporting him from both sides. Hunter stayed behind to provide covering fire while they moved uphill. Another machine gun opened fire from downtrail. Hunter returned fire as he backed away. The bullets were going well over his head and didn't worry him at all.

Thirty meters uptrail he ran into his patrol again, standing stock still. These men had been the target of the high-firing enemy machine gun, the same fire that had comforted Hunter. Someone said, "Musto is dead —a bullet got him in the neck." They were all huddled around the body. "Get moving!" Hunter yelled at them. "Get moving! So Musto is dead. You can't help him. Leave the body. Do you all want to die on this spot?" The others took off at a run; Hunter and Brown took it slow as they half-carried Keller up the ridge.

Hunter called for an air strike against the ground where the elaborate ambush had been rigged. The strike came in too low and was driven off by more machine-gun fire. So Hunter called for a "dustoff" (medical evacuation) Huey to evacuate his wounded. The Huey was shot down by the guns Hunter had just assaulted. It crashed near the river while Hunter and the others watched. The crew escaped, badly shaken but otherwise unhurt. They came, limping, to the American hill position.

The NVA by then was withdrawing toward the southwest; through his binoculars, Hunter could see many men in movement. He could also see, about 400 meters off in the low ground, one Vietnamese perched high in a tree who was looking in Hunter's direction through glasses. More fighter planes had been called for by the battalion.

Halfway down the hill, Sergeant Turner, who has a fair paunch and a walrus moustache—he looks not unlike Bruce Bairnsfather's Old Bill—was engaging in a psywar (psychological warfare) mission. Standing in the clear approximately the distance of a city block from him stood a figure in khaki, wavering and uncertain. Taking out his phrase book, Turner implored the Vietnamese to come in. Nothing happened. Then a napalm pod flamed high just above where the figure had stopped and the Viet soldier vanished in smoke. Turner almost wept. He said mournfully, "I tried to keep him from being cooked and he wouldn't listen." It was not mock sentiment; he was inconsolable. A second dose of napalm from the Air Force finished the observer in the tree.

There were more delayed postludes to both company fights. At 1230 Captain Jones sent out patrols in all directions. They found the countryside completely free of enemy forces. Hunter's second group probed deep. One thousand meters distant, they found the enemy mortar position. It looked as if it had been set there for some time, or at least used now and then, awaiting the night that Americans would come to this particular hill.

In Charley Company, Noble told Lieutenant Maxham to extract his platoon via the village some time around mid-morning. Noble was still dizzy from concussion; a frag had hit his steel pot. The Third Squad, under S.Sgt. Willie T. C. Williams of New Orleans, served as the pivot of the sweep through the ruins, and the other squads, according to Willie, "worked around us in a sort of pinwheeling motion." The enemy had removed most of the bodies from the knoll. Amid the ruins were found five enemy dead, the bodies sprawled grotesquely, as if they had gone down clutching arms and been stripped of them after they had stiffened. The engineer squad was blowing up a 125-foot mahogany, to clear a space for the Hueys to complete the medical evacuation. It was a bad calculation. The tree fell in the wrong direction, killing one of Maxham's boys, Pfc. Charles Coleman, by breaking his neck; then the tree rolled a hundred feet down the slope, mowing flat a bamboo thicket before coming to rest. A more futile death for a rifleman is beyond imagining.

Six weeks later, Hunter took a Huey flight back to the

scene of the fight, to see what he could see. One Vietnamese body had been buried conspicuously in an ornately decorated grave; the hole must have contained a factotum. Some corpses lay there, still ripe for picking by the carrion birds of the place, while elsewhere piles of blackened bones marked where men had been. It was, as Hunter said, "a stinking little pilgrimage."

A few weeks later and he was dead, this rather slight, aggressive, outspoken and soldierly Virginian, who was as good as they come. One more fight and his luck ran out, as it usually does with such men.

Both Lt. Col. David H. Hackworth, my working partner, and I got to know this boy well, had a personal fondness for him, and a deep respect for the depth of his mind and the nobility of his spirit. I remember well that earnest young face and the well-controlled, low-pitched voice, with its overtone of melancholy. On the day when, in front of his soldiers, I asked him how he felt about his first fight, Hunter had responded by quoting from "Dover Beach" the familiar lines by Matthew Arnold:

"And we are here as on a darkling plain
Swept with confused alarms of struggle and
   flight,
Where ignorant armies clash by night."

That was all he said. The words came simply, naturally, and his men did not seem to think it odd. They nodded, even as they had done when he had spoken up voluntarily in fierce condemnation of the M-16 rifle.

Hunter was a soldier thoroughly in command of himself, and to others who willingly followed him he gave his own tone. The Georgia lass to whom he was affianced later wrote me, "Americans do not realize . . . that in Vietnam we are losing the best of our young men as England lost Rupert Brooke and others in World War I.''

She was right about the boy who didn't return, and she saw the Army to which he belonged simply as an extension of the person she knew and loved so well. As to the sense of duty binding one man to another over there, it was not too high a tribute.

Come the Foxes————————

When the company started its long march at 0800, moving northeast from Hill 637 in the hope of bivouacking at Hill 292, all hands were content with one thing—the man on the point for Second Platoon.

That was a phenomenon compounded, because the point man is the eyes, ears, and nose of an infantry column thrusting into enemy country; if his senses fail, so may the unit. Yet Spec. 4 David E. McLemore, age 19, had been with the company only five weeks.

More about him later. The unit was Charley Company, Second Battalion of the 35th Regiment, 25th Infantry Division, under command of Capt. Michael R. Tryon, age 25.

The day was 28 October, 1966, and it turned out to be hot and fair, a dazzling sun boosting the temperature above 80 before mid-morning, with not one cloud appearing in the sky thereafter.

The scene was the western Central Highlands. The march, should one wish to be technical about it, was to extend from coordinate YA 778-567 to coordinate 796-597 on the same map sheet. It was over rough country—straight-faced, slab-sided hills for the most part, with interspersed jungle patches, the canopy of which occasionally rose to 70 feet, the undergrowth so dense that the column front had to hack its way through, though there was little bamboo and no bamboozles (great snarled clumps of the stuff at ground level) whatever.

The mission was to "search and destroy," a military euphemism meaning that, if any enemy force gets in the way, it is to be bopped. If nothing of the sort transpired, the column might link up with Task Force MacDonald, a name that sounds big, though the TF consisted of a headquarters company, recon platoon, and an understrength C.I.D.G. (Civilian Irregular Defense Group) company, all under command of Capt. Michael MacDonald, USMA '62. The TF was about five kilometers east of Tryon's outfit, and both bodies were beating out the countryside directly north of the Se San River.

Expectations were not high. No promising or specific piece of intelligence had pointed them in the direction taken. Still, they went heavily loaded. The average rifleman carried 500 rounds for his M-16, two frag grenades, and one smoke grenade. Some toted as many as four frag grenades and three smoke grenades besides the rifle ammo. There were two claymore mines per squad. Fountain, a machine gunner, was loaded with 900 rounds for his M-60. Marsh, a grenadier, had his M-79 launcher, 50 rounds to fire from it, a .45 Colt pistol with 40 rounds, and, at the last moment, added five canister rounds to the 50 high explosive rounds that he was already packing for the M-79. A human pack mule, he must have been burdened with 70 pounds (not counting the clothing he wore), with almost no chance that he would need even half of it.

The variation was greatest in the food department. Some men carried three rations. Others had none, or a

fraction of one. Those who went foodless were big
eaters who had already downed everything they brought
to the field.

So we get to McLemore, the point man. He carried
520 rifle rounds and half a ration, well-conditioned to
heft the one and do without the other. He is a tall, handsome Negro, with the build of an all-American end. A
high school graduate from Fort Worth, he had starred
in football, baseball, and track. For other reasons, perhaps better ones, he stands out in the crowd. A member
of a motor unit, he had volunteered for infantry duty.
Then, in the brief time he had been with the unit, he had
memorized the full name and home town of every one
of its 129 members. He radiated self-confidence and
some special quality in him, possibly his quiet manner
and directness of statement, won the trust of all the
other men. So he was quickly made an acting NCO.
There is no explaining his prodigious memory. He had
no special training; he had worked only in a metal-
processing plant while going to school. One can imagine
such a man going far in politics.

It proved to be not a big day for McLemore on the
point, or for Second Platoon, which slogged along
behind him, or for First Platoon, which had stepped out
earlier and was at least 1,000 meters away throughout
the march, or for Third Platoon, which moved separately from Second by about the same distance. They
did not move by the same trace, nor did any platoon
hold to one azimuth. They had been told to zigzag to
confuse the enemy, and they followed instructions.
Also, they had been warned to stay away from trails "as
much as possible." But, as things went, much wasn't
possible. There were too many trails, all could not be
avoided, and, as men grew tired, the temptation to take

a trail rather than to hack through thick brush became less resistible.

Without incident of any kind, the morning march was simply a sweat, bone-wearying, nervously irritating, and blister-forming. The only open country the men saw were a few rice paddy strips, most of them completely dried out, the few under cultivation badly tended. Not a person was to be seen. Otherwise, their route carried them alternately through narrow flats thickly grown with elephant grass, brush, or reeds, and over the sharp ridges, rock-ledged at the base and halfway up the slope, crowned with jungle growth spliced heavily with wait-a-minute thorn vines and creepers.

At 1100 they entered upon a well-used enemy base camp. Their early caution was in vain. It had been stripped bare. Its one-time occupants had cleared away, leaving nothing that was worth destroying. But there they rested briefly in the shade. At about 1730 Second Platoon came to a hamlet with four hootches. But the day was going fast, the column still had a far piece to travel, and so McLemore kept going, not pausing to check the village out. One hour earlier, First Platoon had come that way and had stopped for a look.

In two of the houses there were fires, or there had been, and the coals were still warm. In all four there were jugs of water and the taste was sweet. Each had a supply of rice and eggs, with salt and other pantry stuff. Two had henhouses; the chickens were feeding. The nests were checked by the platoon sergeant, Glenn Gladue; there were no newly laid eggs. Outside each house was a foxhole.

One joker commented, "Looka there, foxes next to chicken roosts."

Gladue, the first to sight the houses, said to Lt. James

Lanning, "I would say these are fresh signs."

Lanning nodded.

"What do you think it means?" Gladue asked.

Lanning shook his head.

Gladue subsequently dismissed the subject with a comment appropriate to the entire day's exercise: "That's the one thing about the VC. You can't tell him from a simple farmer, especially when you don't have a chance to see either."

First Platoon moved on 1,000 meters to Hill 292, which had already been designated for the nighttime defense. It closed on the knob at 1700, but did not feel too cheerful about it. The ground was high enough, but there were many tall trees, and the ground was littered with large boulders and rubble, though there were patches of loose earth. The men had time to send out a watering party to a clear stream that lay about 300 meters to the west of the position, some distance beyond the open ground that would be used for a landing zone. By the time the party had returned with the water, First Platoon's third of the perimeter was already well fox-holed, and the crew-served weapons were in place.

McLemore led Second Platoon into the rim just 90 minutes later. Its watering party was sped to the creek because the night was now coming with a rush, as it always does in these latitudes. The rest of the platoon fitted into a sector and began looking for the softer spots where digging was possible.

McLemore saw a relatively tight position, approximately egg-shaped, measuring about 70 by 100 meters, if two lines were drawn through the center, configured so because it followed a crestline overlooking narrow and sloping fields of fire. Although hardly a desirable spot for defense, it was better than the average in Vietnam and was preferable to any other prospect in the neighborhood. However, it was the presetting of the LZ that had determined where the perimeter would form.

Only 29 men were in First Platoon. Second Platoon was also thin, mustering just 31. Counting the men around Tryon in the headquarters group, the force as of that moment totaled 73, which is less than three-fourths of the minimum figure that the experts say is needed for a rifle company to "be in business." Unsatisfactory is the word for it.

The Second Platoon sweep that would go out that evening once the perimeter had shaped up was already standing by, one squad armed and ready to go, but awaiting, as were Captain Tryon and the others, the return of the watering party. The patrol out of First Platoon, under S.Sgt. Jesse Johnson, a 31-year-old Negro from St. Louis with nine years of Regular Army service, had made its round trip, scouting one main trail that ran past the perimeter for 250 meters to the northwest.

"Negative," Johnson had said to Tryon. "We didn't see or smell one thing."

First Platoon's outposts had been pulled in and no LP's had yet gone out.

So among the men of the main body within the clearing there was no general feeling of alarm or awareness of immediate danger. Yet there were exceptions. The dark was coming ever faster, though it was not yet full in those few minutes before the moon would rise. It was the eerie time of day when the imagination plays tricks and the eyes see too much and too little.

Both machine-gun positions in First Platoon were well forward on the rim and the crews, working hard at it, had about finished the task of setting the weapons and digging a hole in very loose earth. Pfc. Michael Edwards, the assistant gunner on the right, straightened up and peered at the brush line 30 meters to his front.

"Surer than hell," he whispered, "I see eyes out there. Can't you see them?"

His audience was the gunner, Pfc. Dennis W. Fountain, 21, of Lansing, Mich. Fountain quit digging to take a look. Several moments passed, then he answered, "I see something that looks like eyes." He paused, looked back over his shoulder, and added, "Mike, the moon has just come over the trees. What we see may be a reflection from the leaves."

At the other gun, Pfc. "Chick" St. Clair, head gunner, was also stirring and staring. "Mac," he whispered, "I'm not kidding—I see something out there. Maybe it's my imagination. You take a look."

McLemore squinted long and hard. "I see nothing," he said. "I hope I keep seeing nothing. You better hope, too."

At that precise moment a whistle was blown somewhere out beyond the company circle. As the sound died, a green-star cluster rose above the bush not more than 10 meters to their front.

Among the watering party, now legging it back to the company position as fast as men could beat through the bush, there were none of these equivocal doubts and false hopes. Approaching the landing zone on the return journey, Pfc. Gary Lynn Finney was certain he saw a movement off to his right, and told the others. Finney, a 23-year-old welder from Bay City, Mich., the father of two children, may have felt a pang that he had extended his tour in Vietnam for six months.

As they swept past the LZ, they all felt the presence. They saw no one and heard nothing. But the reeds on both sides of them were bending and billowing, and they knew the movement marked the passage of crawling men because the night was windless. The perimeter was

50 meters farther along. Wordlessly, and by common consent, the men broke into a run. Spec. 4 James E. Pell, who had charge of the Command Post security detail, rushed on ahead to tell the news to 1st Sgt. Huey P. Danley, a Louisianan. Not quite making it, he was five meters from Danley when the first hot rounds beat against the company's ground.

One casualty was calling for an aid man before the bullets arrived. Pfc. Terry Kellam, a rifleman, had been standing when the green-star cluster was fired. It hit him in the chest and shoulder. Pfc. Thomas V. Browne, a 19-year-old high school grad from Denver, serving as assistant gunner, tried to help by saying, "You got a nice Purple Heart burn." That was small consolation for Kellam, and there was none for Browne. He had eaten all his rations much too early during the march, and his belly was feeling empty.

Less than 30 seconds later came the blast of rifle and machine-gun fire. It broke more raggedly than shatteringly against the half of the company circle that faced the LZ, engaging all positions of Second Platoon and three positions of First Platoon. Blazing at them were two machine guns and perhaps 20 other automatic weapons. The North Vietnamese fire base was at least 30 meters from the company line as the action began. This is a greater distance than is their custom in staging a surprise. Sergeant Johnson kept wondering about it. Had the rush-through of the watering party spoiled what the enemy had intended?

Certainly something—whether it was the dash of the watering party or some deranging element known only to themselves—must have made the enemy charge in planlessly, and without first reconning their target. For, in staging it, this was a fool's exercise. They engaged entirely and directly half of the one platoon that was solidly set, while at first striking hardly more than a glancing blow against the platoon that was footloose and unprotected. And on the far side of the oval was open, unguarded ground, a broad and inviting avenue, where other troops should have been.

They—the enemy—had come over the same trail from the southwest that Second Platoon had taken from the hamlet; had, in effect, shadowed the column for that distance, then lost themselves in the tall grass when they saw the watering party doubling back toward their rear. All things that happened that evening, and every sign that was studied on the following morning, so indicate. Whether the shadowing had begun much earlier in the day is beyond saying. There is only the mute proof suggesting that the people in the little settlement had been warned in time to clear away. Yet that had happened 90 minutes before Second Platoon came up, a circumstance that implies the NVA was somewhere in the vicinity and had latched onto the company's movement rather late in the day.

Seeing the opening act from another angle, Mc-Lemore was still more mystified than Johnson. Enemy skirmishers had gained to within 10 meters of his position when the first round was fired. He could see them dodging about now in the underbrush, lunging here and there for better cover, though they were not shooting. Although McLemore's own M-60 was chattering away, the ground dropped off so sharply just beyond the muzzle that he could not bring fire to bear on these dodging figures without standing, and he figured that that would be a silly way to die. He said to his partner, St. Clair, "Click, we're throwing away bullets."

Sergeant Wendell Wilson of Second Platoon, from Scottsville, Ky., was killed instantly in the first second. He had been sitting, back to the enemy, feet dangling in a shallow hole, as he spooned beans from a C-ration tin. Two bullets, not more than an inch apart, entered near his spine and tore through his heart. He slumped over, doubled up in the foxhole.

Seeing it happen, not five feet away, Fountain knew Wilson was dead and did not bother to check the body. At the same time, Pfc. Aaron Cowan of East St. Louis, a rifleman on the other side of Fountain, was hit by a bullet in the left thigh. Bewildered by the suddenness of the wounding, he yelled to Fountain, "Hell, they didn't let me get started."

Private First Class Evander Marsh, a 20-year-old Negro from Newark, had time to get off two rounds from his M-79 launchers; he aimed toward the spot 15 meters off where he had seen the flare go up. The reason he had taken position behind a tree was that he had found too late that the foxhole was not large enough to hold both himself and his buddy, Pfc. Thomas Leak Jr. of Kansas City, Mo. So he yielded the better cover to his friend and within 30 seconds afterward heard Leak crying, "I'm hit, Marsh, hit, hit, hit." Marsh crawled over from the tree. Leak had a bad sucking chest wound from a bullet. "You'll have to wait," Marsh said. "The medic has his hands full." Starting back to the tree, Marsh ran into Pfc. George Thomas, a rifleman. A bullet had creased Thomas' left shoulder blade; it was a slight wound. Thomas was crawling to his position to get his rifle, though he had no intention of using it. He said to Marsh, "I been shot through and through. I'm finished."

Browne, the assistant gunner, had no sooner finished giving aid to Kellam than he heard a cry from his own position: "Oh, my eye, my eye, my eye." It came from the chief gunner, Spec. 4 Robert Martinez of Denver. A grenade fragment had blinded his left eye. Browne pulled out his handkerchief and handed it to Martinez, saying, "That will have to do you till the aid man comes." Together, they kept working the gun, firing at the flashes they saw in the bush. Careful with their aiming, they fired not more than 100 rounds in the first minute and were enormously pleased when they saw some of the flashes from enemy ground wink out, to stay that way.

Sergeant Johnson was also having his moments of satisfaction. When the fight had been going less than one minute, he crawled along, checking the platoon line from end to end. Every man in position to fire was using his weapon.

In Second Platoon's sector both machine guns were going, and one was going too well. Whereas young Fountain was firing in short bursts, Pfc. Glenn Young on the other gun was letting everything go. "Slow down a bit," Fountain yelled to him. "Take it easy, save that ammo." Young shouted back, "OK, I will," and just then a bullet hit him in the right shoulder. Badly hurt, he slumped over and rested on the gun, waiting for an aid man.

By the time the fight was three minutes along Captain Tryon became concerned that the men on the embattled sector were firing excessively, though somewhat less than half of the perimeter remained nonengaged. He sent Sergeant Danley over from the command post with instructions to crawl along the foxhole line and pass the word: "Ease off on the fire; make it semiautomatic." Then for emphasis, the captain himself yelled it loud and clear: "Fire semiautomatic!"

Finney, who was working as radio telephone operator for the captain, got the word along to the others. And he also heard the echo. Back from the bush where the enemy lay came the mocking cry in good English:

"That's right, boys. Make it semiautomatic, not automatic. Do what your captain says." The enemy is funny that way. Other voices from the bush were chorusing: "Hello, hello, hello, hello," chattering along like so many magpies.

With the fight only five minutes along McLemore tested the claymore mines he had buried and found that the wire had been cut, which could only mean that skirmishers had moved to within 15 feet of him. Thereupon Edwards tested his claymore and in the wake of the blast heard several voices screaming only a few yards to his front. He had fired the mine in the nick of time.

His partner, Fountain, was reserving his mine for the big push that he thought would be coming soon. A cool head this one, though he is so slight and so blond that the nickname Baby Face would fit him. Fountain worked on the Oldsmobile assembly line before becoming a soldier. Married to a girl from Remus, Mich., he got news that their first child, Laurie Linn, was born at just about the time of this battle. It was his first action and he was making the most of it. He knew that there were enemy skirmishers within 10 feet of his gun, but, like McLemore, he could not bring fire to bear on them without standing in the clear.

Fountain's first good opening came when a figure bounded out of the dark and straight for the gun where Young had collapsed from the shoulder wound. Before Fountain could swing his M-60 around, the Vietnamese, standing directly above Young, put two more bullets in him, one in the right leg, the other in the left chest. So died Young, much too young. The skirmisher started back over the piled-up logs in front of Young's gun. He was standing again and starting to run when Fountain's M-60 fire cut him down.

By then—five minutes after the fight began—artillery

was supporting the American infantry. The lines were too close-joined to permit effective help by killing shells, so the guns were firing only illuminating rounds. The flares made the foreground almost as bright as sunlight would have, but they were also falling so close that the defenders were almost blinded.

For the first time McLemore could clearly see five enemy soldiers crawling toward his position. His partner, St. Clair, taking a chance, jumped up and shot three of them with the M-60—range, seven feet. A fourth skirmisher, five feet to the trio's left, which put him on McLemore's right, jumped to his feet, SKS carbine in hand with shining bayonet fixed, and came on.

He was moving on a diagonal, passing up St. Clair. McLemore had moved a few feet away when St. Clair was firing. Spec. 4 Allan Jarrett, now standing in his foxhole, yelled to McLemore, "Mac, he's charging you!" But McLemore, for the moment, could see nothing; he had been blinded by the flares. Without taking aim, Jarrett fired an M-79 grenade at the man. The range was too close; the grenade bounced off his chest without exploding, giving him no pause whatsoever. Jarrett dropped his M-79, whipped out his Colt .45, and emptied the clip at the charging figure. At least four bullets hit the Vietnamese around the chest and shoulders and part of his jaw was shot away. Yet not one bullet dropped him and he kept coming, though a little slower. McLemore was now with it; his eyesight had adjusted and he could see the target in silhouette. He emptied a full magazine from his M-16 into the enemy soldier. The shots tore his guts out—McLemore saw the abdominal cavity open and the intestines spill forth —but he still was not stopped. The Viet dropped to one knee, paused for a second or two, rose, and came on again. McLemore emptied two more magazines in him

as he tottered forward. The man dropped at Mc-
Lemore's feet, a bloody pulp, riddled by more than 50
bullets. Even so, the American had had to step back
several paces as the Vietnamese came on to avoid collision.

"He got to kissin' distance," said McLemore, shaking.

"Did you ever see anything like that?" St. Clair remarked.

To both of them it seemed that in that moment they
had played out an act quite alone, an act in which no
other person in the world had the slightest interest.
Looking at the bayonet and the smashed SKS, Mc-
Lemore shook his head in surprise at himself that he had
blown so much ammunition.

After six minutes of the action it seemed to Finney
that the ground beyond the perimeter suddenly quieted.
Then he heard a whistle blow, and as the sound died two
grenades came in on his machine gun. Both were duds.
He waited a few seconds before throwing them out, then
he heard grenades popping elsewhere along the line.
Eight potato mashers sailed in on McLemore and St.
Clair; all failed to explode. Marsh was less fortu-
nate. He was diving head first for his foxhole when the
grenade shower started. His legs were in the air when
one potato masher exploded five feet from the hole.
One slug tore into his kneecap.

Private First Class Timothy Rooney, First Platoon's
aid man, was next to Second Platoon's flank when the
grenading began. One missile blasted out next to his
legs; miraculously, no metal touched him, though the
explosion lifted him bodily and threw him outside the
perimeter. In the fall he pulled the muscles of his left
arm. Crawling back, he started toward Martinez to give
him first aid. A North Vietnamese charged in to stop

him, flashing a knife. Rooney took out his .45 pistol, got to his feet, grappled with the man, then conked him in the head and continued on, paying as much heed as if he had been swatting a fly. Finney then saw someone flash out of the darkness and empty an M-16 clip into the prone figure. Rooney was already working on Martinez.

Private First Class James Stewart, a Second Platoon rifleman, was lying next to a tree and using it for cover. As he rolled over, a grenade came in and exploded under his body. The metal tore into his groin, scrotum, and lower bowel. Rooney looked him over and figured he had little or no chance. He gave him morphine. Sgt. Phillip Hord, a First Platoon squad leader, had a grenade explode in front of his foxhole and was peppered with metal in the chest and shoulders. Also out of First Platoon, Spec. 4 James Springer was hit by fragments in the back and right arm; this happened less than a minute after a bullet, first stripping the sight from his rifle, became lodged in his right arm.

Fighting next to McLemore, Pfc. Harry Williams was hit by a large grenade shard in the right thigh. "Mac," he said, "I think I got a bullet in my leg." McLemore stripped down his pants, felt him over, and said, "So far as I can tell, you got nothing there but blood." A minute or so later, Rooney was in the hole bandaging Williams. It was his first fight.

The grenading lasted about four minutes. By the time the fight was 10 minutes along, the U.S. artillery was working over the ground outside the perimeter, feeling its way carefully, gradually coming closer, firing three shells at a time. The light battery support came from A and B of the Second of the Ninth Field. There was also fire from the 175's of A/6/14th, based at Pleijerang. Guided by Lt. James Stutts, a forward observer who had been promoted that day, the fires ranged all around the outer circle, except in the south-southwest quadrant.

There was good reason for the omission. The company's Third Platoon was still out there somewhere, wondering what to do. With the fight 11 minutes old, the platoon called in for the first time. It had held up at a river bank, and was approximately 700 meters from the perimeter to the south-southwest. What to do? "Don't try to come in," Tryon said. "Stay right where you are until morning." With the pressure still building against the company, that was the toughest decision made during the night, and its wisdom is beyond question. The platoon stayed in place. One man was killed by a sniper in early morning; its experience otherwise was uneventful.

When the grenading tapered off, Pfc. John M. Mucci saw a large figure loom directly in front of his foxhole. Because of its size, he thought he was looking at a GI. "Come on in!" Mucci yelled. The figure dashed toward him. A little late, Mucci realized it was a North Vietnamese. He tried to fire upward with his M-16; there was only a click—the magazine was empty. He made a football tackle at the man's knees and dragged him down into the foxhole. Mucci had already reached for his machete as he now slashed away at the tall enemy.

Specialist 4 Robert Prunier jumped to help Mucci and got a throttling hold on the NVA soldier's neck. Suddenly Mucci's blade broke, leaving half the steel in the man's shoulder. Prunier, maintaining his stranglehold, was now on top of the Vietnamese and bearing down on him with his full weight. Mucci, freeing himself from the tangle, picked up Prunier's M-16. By then Prunier had the body so well covered that Mucci had only the man's legs for a target. He fired two bullets into the thighs and the figure went limp.

Figuring he was dead, Mucci and Prunier picked him up out of the foxhole and heaved him toward the outer darkness. The body came down heavily on the back of the aid man, Rooney. Rooney grabbed for one arm and was astounded to see it swing around in a complete circle; Mucci's machete had cut through the bone and the arm was dangling by flesh alone.

Sickened, believing the man dead, Rooney started crawling away. Mucci, meanwhile, had lost interest, having resumed fire from his foxhole. He glanced that way just by chance and saw that the "dead man," too, was in motion, pawing his way along, using only one arm. That was too much. Having used everything else, Mucci went after him with an entrenching shovel, at last killing the enemy by bashing in his head. It took two or three minutes.

Maybe a minute passed after Mucci got back to his foxhole. Then from the outer darkness came a mocking voice in English: "Hey GI, how is your company commander?"

Undaunted, Mucci sang out, "He's fine. How about yours?"

"Not very well," came the answer. "You have just killed him."

There could be little doubt about it. What had once been a fine figure of a man was ornamented with an officer's belt and was carrying a pistol that had remained undrawn, its firing pin broken.

With that incident, the curtain dropped, concluding the first act. Beginning at approximately 1930 there came a quiet that lasted for 30 minutes. Preceding it, a derisive yell came from in front of McLemore: "Hey GI's, we are backing away. But don't worry. We will be back. So don't go yet."

But unlike the effect of Chinese Communist music on

Gen. Walton Walker's Eighth Army in Korea in November, 1950, these bizarre and macabre touches to the enemy's behavior neither awed nor added special tension to the Americans present who were fighting the NVA for the first time. McLemore, Fountain, and the others talked it over. They concluded that the enemy was "hopped up" from some narcotic. There was another mark of it; the enemy were pressing the attack very indifferently. They had numbers but no unity, signals but no system, madness but no method.

How far the North Vietnamese had pulled back, no one knew, and, in the circumstances, there was no thought of scouting after them to find out. Tryon and the others around the command post had their hands full too soon afterward. Two Air Force Husky medical-evacuation craft were being brought in to take out the most critical cases among the casualties. Spec. 4 Clarence Young was on the radio, talking the lead Husky into the proper spot; he would shortly be relieved by Finney. Other men were moving around inside the perimeter, waving flashlights, or ready to throw out flares to illuminate the scene. The company simply risked it that the enemy had withdrawn far enough and would stay away long enough.

The lead Husky made it to the right spot and dropped its hook. An Air Force aid man slid down the cable and joined the men on the ground. With his help, Cowan, Martinez, and Leak, all critically wounded in the first minute of the fight, were made comfortable and lifted up to the Husky in that order. It took about 10 minutes.

Then the Husky made a sudden lurch and the cable got snagged in the treetops. Captain Tryon came running to help free it, tugged hard for several minutes, and at last yelled to Finney, "Everything's OK now!" Finney put it over the radio telephone: "You are free."

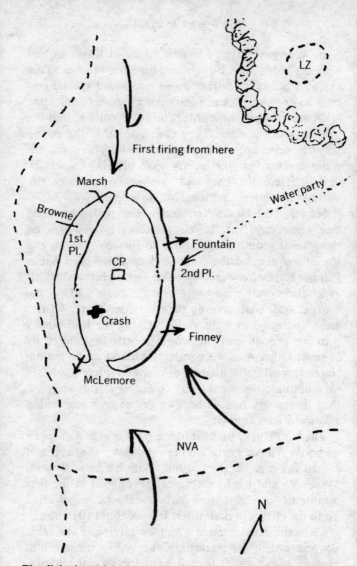

LZ

First firing from here

Marsh

Browne

1st. Pl.

CP

Crash

McLemore

Water party

Fountain

2nd Pl.

Finney

NVA

N

The fight in which the Husky crashed. Positions of men and platoons are indicated. Arrows show attacks and counterfire around U.S. perimeter.

But the air medic was still on the ground, so the pilot tarried. Tryon came running to Finney, shouting, "Tell them to get out. They have been here far too long." Finney didn't get a chance to relay the message.

Sergeant Johnson was at his position along the perimeter, paying no attention to the Husky. From about 20 meters to his front, he saw a rocket rise from the ground, moving slowly at first, almost vertically. One of his riflemen fired a burst of tracers that way. Johnson yelled, "Look out!" and jumped outside the perimeter to get a better view of the course of the rocket, a Soviet-made RPG-7.

Finney saw it coming. The Husky was hovering about 15 feet above the treetops, roughly perpendicular to the command post. The rocket exploded into the trees, maybe 20 feet below the helicopter, but the trajectory was dead on and the full force of the explosion blew upward into the aircraft. The Husky came nosedown, at first gently, as if making a normal descent to a landing zone. Finney thought to himself, "They're going to do it."

Browne, the gunner, was in a foxhole, directly under the falling Husky. He, Spec. 4 Ronald Blank, and Pfc. Earl Huff, followed the rocket in flight, looking upward. They saw the explosion and all jumped together to clear away from the collision area. They made 10 feet, then were mowed down and swept aside by a great tree limb that, falling, bounced them out of the perimeter, knocking them cold.

Finney, eyes riveted on the Husky, saw it sheer off to the right when 30 feet above ground and crash into the trees. He jumped up and ran blindly. The dying craft hit earth exactly where he had been sitting, its body closing down over the command post foxhole.

That put the wreck just 20 meters from the hole where

Evander Marsh lay. Sergeant Hord yelled, "Run! Run" and jumped from the hole. But George Thomas, wounded and down, was also there. Marsh knew he couldn't run. So Marsh made his choice, stayed in the hole, and covered Thomas' body with his own. The sacrifice nearly cooked him.

The Husky was already burning when the drop started and the rush of the descent worked on the fire like an updraft, so that when the craft struck earth with the nose wedging between two trees the flames were already licking toward the high branches. Being at dead center, the pyre illuminated every corner of the perimeter. The men—and most of them stayed put in their positions—could feel the heat in the farthest foxholes.

"It was like daylight all around us," they said.

McLemore had been picking up grenades, his back to the scene, when the crash came. Assisting him in the tidying-up chore was his platoon commander, Lt. Ramon T. Pulliam, an Alabaman, who was standing and looking the other way.

McLemore heard Pulliam scream, "God damn! God damn! God damn!" the voice rising higher each time. Those few seconds contained more horror than Pulliam had known in his entire life and he was momentarily paralyzed. Then the white Alabaman turned back to the big Negro from Texas, whacked him on the back, and yelled, "Mac, for God's sake, get in there and fight it!"

Pulliam was already off and running toward the blazing Husky. One other volunteer was ahead of him, Cpl. Clyde Shell, an artillery forward observer. As they moved in, all other sounds were drowned out by the chorus of screaming from inside the ship.

Sergeant Johnson also jumped from his foxhole and came on the run to join the rescue party. Next came Rooney, the boy medic who had already been through the ordeal of a lifetime in one evening.

Shell ran for the crew compartment, blistered his hand in coping with the panel, but somehow managed to force the opening. He grabbed the crew chief by the hands to yank him out. The man was a torch and already burning to death. His flesh came off in Shell's hands. Shell fell back to earth as the figure, convulsively, fell over backwards inside.

McLemore stood next to him with an entrenching tool, heaving dirt on the fire, shoveling like a madman. His mind had closed out all but one thought, even that of danger; he had to keep fighting the blaze so long as there was a chance to get anyone out. That was how he toiled for 10 minutes, while his hands blistered—beyond all fear for his own safety.

Pulliam and Johnson worked as a team at the front of the fire. The Husky's plexiglass had been shattered by the crash, a fact that helped to feed the fire, though it was a blessing in disguise. They could get to the pilots. Johnson had grabbed the air medic's ax. With Pulliam helping him, he used it to cut away the pilot's harness. Then they pulled him out, his clothing ablaze, a small problem left to other hands. For they were already back, struggling to save the co-pilot, first cutting the harness, then hauling him bodily through the aperture. It was not easy. A large man, he was in dementia from his physical agony and resisted with a giant's strength.

Rooney looked him over and passed judgment. The man was so badly burned about the neck and mouth that he was losing the fight to keep breathing. The one chance was to perform what Rooney called a tracheotomy, but what was in fact a cricothyroidotomy.

The co-pilot still lashed out wildly when anyone tried to touch him. Somehow they got him down on the ground and laid him behind one of the tallest trees, about two rods from the plane. But that did not subdue him. McLemore was the largest and strongest soldier present. Pulliam told him that he would have to take on the job. So McLemore tried to hold the man still, covering him with his own body. It was next to impossible. He kept screaming through a mask of blood and dirt, breaking off the scream now and then only to gasp for air. His spasmatic writhing was like that of an epileptic in a fit, and when his hands broke free he tried to beat on McLemore's face. The Negro was tossed this way and that, with Rooney trying to help him.

The struggle went on for 20 minutes before the co-pilot quieted. Midway, the Husky blew up. The explosion spread flaming gasoline over McLemore's back as he covered the man. It also set Rooney afire and hurled him up against the big tree, stunning him. Both returned to their work, badly burned, weakened. Now Pulliam and Shell had to take a hand, as did Spec. 5 George Kraklio, the senior medic.

The operation was performed. The whole thing had been hopeless from the beginning. Soon after, the co-pilot died.

More ironic still, Cowan, Martinez, and Leak, the three soldiers who were shot before they had a chance to fight, all burned to death in the Husky.

Tryon, through the crisis, had been doing as a good commander should—moving around the circle from position to position, talking to the men, steadying them. The captain was certain the enemy would come back, and because this conviction never left him he continued with his rounds throughout the night.

A few shots from snipers hidden in the outer darkness kicked up dirt within the company circle during these minutes. Men wondered then, and wonder still, why this strange enemy did not return in strength in that catastrophic hour when, morally and physically, the defenders were completely vulnerable. Every fighting position was under high light, and the crash of the Husky had shocked, stunned, and demoralized a rifle company that had gone through a grisly fire fight undismayed. The failure to seize the opening was but another lunatic reaction, as baffling as the aberrant actions of the individual skirmishers.

There is proof of a negative kind that the enemy had not pulled far away and were not yet headed for base camp when the explosion took place. At 0300 a slow drizzle began falling, and shortly thereafter a light ground fog from the bottoms shrouded the perimeter. Visibility was reduced to about five meters. The sniping ceased about then. A more pressing requirement had taken over because the opportunity had arisen. The enemy came back in strength to collect bodies.

Finney had shot one sniper out of a tree within the perimeter. The Vietnamese fell 40 feet, landed on his head, and broke his neck.

McLemore had shot a second man next to his foxhole—not more than eight feet away—emptying half a magazine in his chest before he fell. For five minutes he watched him die under the lights.

Then there was the officer whom Mucci and Prunier had worked over, who had given them such a hard time, and the hard charger whom McLemore and Jarrett had together killed, this within the perimeter.

None of these bodies were there when morning came. On the slope, St. Clair had mowed down three men with his machine gun and the bodies still lay there when the Husky burned; by morning light, one body remained.

Here and there lay a corpse that the enemy had overlooked in the dark and the fog. They counted 16 all told, and officially reported a "body count" of 19, so slight an exaggeration that it was more than a little bit honest.

But that was not why they felt so low when they marched toward the landing zone a little later in the day, shortly after Sergeant Johnson had taken out a sweep to the northwest of the perimeter. It had been good hunting. The patrol had run into three NVA soldiers where they lay sleeping on a rock, killed the men, and got their weapons, two AK-47 rifles and a machine gun. That gave Johnson his moment of bitter satisfaction. Second Platoon, on its sweep, had done as well, capturing two NVA prisoners.

Even so, as the men of Charley Company moved on, they spoke their regret that they had ever seen this field. Johnson said why:

"We had it made. Our fight was won. We had all done well. And we knew it. Successfully, we got our worst wounded off. We felt relief. Our hearts were high. Then the Husky was shot down and we plunged to despair with it. I felt like a part of me had died."

Some months after the action reported here, David McLemore was killed in battle. Though I did not hear of it until much later, I wrote his mother, Elizabeth McLemore of Forth Worth. From her letter in reply, which was moving throughout, the following several sentences, at the least, are appropriate to this writing:

"We know that David not only died for his country; during his short time in service, he won many wonderful friends. I, being his Mother, have some special reason to feel proud. I taught David to be a kind and respectable person. I know now it was not all in vain."

A Small Problem—————
————————of Command

The Plei Trap Valley is a pocket of land roughly 10 by 20 miles, belonging to South Vietnam and projecting into Cambodia.

The Se San River describes the boundary between the two nations on its southern side. There are mountains along the east and west borders. Although the valley proper is relatively flat, it narrows at the northern extremity to a tightly constricted pass. The floor of the valley is overgrown for most of the 20 miles north to south with triple-canopied jungle, its tallest trees standing 200 feet or more. The undergrowth is as dense as any in Southeast Asia. No nice place, but neatly named, it was never intended by nature as a freeway for maneuvering armies. For the valley was, in effect, a salient jutting into enemy-used country, which tactically gave the other camp the main advantage, only marginally offset by air mobility. Why should anyone wish to fight when the odds are wrong? It is a good question.

Here was the little theater for the playlet already begun, with much shouting, stamping, and reading of signals out of the wings. A many-act affair and long-drawn, it exemplifies how large operations in Vietnam derive less from a plan than from patience in working over jigsaw puzzles.

The first rumbles were heard by Lt. Col. Eleazar Parmly IV on 1 October, 1966. Here is a name out of history, Eleazar the First having been a distinguished president of Dartmouth College. His great-grandson graduated from West Point in 1946. By this time 41 years old, redheaded, slender, in prime physical shape, and one of the most outspoken Army officers extant, he was with Special Forces and in overall command of the C.I.D.G. camps at Du Co, Plei Me, and Pleijerang, the far west of the Central Highlands.

Parmly learned that one of his camps would be knocked off by the NVA "in an effort to influence elections in the United States," and that the likely pigeon was Du Co. The warning filtered down through intelligence channels. There were other details, more precise, possibly more sinister. The North Vietnamese Army plan also had arranged that any reaction (relief) forces, rushing to help the pigeon, would be mousetrapped. It was spelled out that the 630th NVA Front (such high numbers are purposed to startle and shock) was just across the border in Cambodia, which meant the 32nd NVA Division, with the 32nd, 33rd, and 88th Regiments. The 24th Regiment was thought to be somewhere in the center of Kontum Province. Another still spicier detail, the 630th Front was reported to be supplied with 105-mm. mountain artillery, Red Chinese advisers, and Red Chinese service units.

Parmly pondered these things, but he didn't believe them. There was no special reason for doubt. It was merely that some field service and the reading of sitreps (situation reports) had confirmed his skepticism, an attitude congenial to his nature. The fix seemed unlikely, but then war isn't a likely business.

However, high authority was also reading the same mail and possibly worrying more. If anything went gravely wrong west of Pleiku and Kontum, the buck would certainly pass to the U.S. Fourth Infantry Division. Thus, it was decided to harden the Du Co camp by positioning U.S. tanks and artillery there; at the same time, the road to Du Co (Highway No. 19) would be improved and secured by Fourth Division soldiers. All Special Forces personnel under Parmly, while the crisis lasted, would be put under Brig. Gen. Glenn Walker, ADC (assistant division commander) of Fourth Division, a practical-minded dirt soldier. At the same time, one batallion of the U.S. 25th Infantry Division was displaced north into General Collins' command, to beef it up for a possible emergency.

In all of this was much wasted motion. The Du Co camp would never become pressed. Nor would Plei Me, rated the second most likely target. Infantrymen of the Fourth and Twenty-Fifth Divisions prowled all around these camps and found nothing.

Colonel Williams, the lanky, saturnine, and methodical G-2 (Army intelligence officer) serving Lt. Gen. "Swede" Larsen at the II Corps zone headquarters in Nha Trang, was mulling over a swatch of reports covering fresh signs of NVA hustle and bustle along the Cambodian frontier, but reaching no more positive conclusion about their meaning than Parmly.

On 10 October, two line-crossing agents reported locating a brand-new one-thousand-bed NVA hospital just inside the Cambodian border on a line even with Pleiku. The discounting of such a report is automatic: thousand-bed hospitals are rare the world over.

That same day, a large enemy rice-carrying party was intercepted by a patrol three or so miles northeast of the Pleijerang camp.

The same patrol, extending the mission, found 68 sampans, rafts, and other water craft, uncamouflaged, moored to the bank of the nigh side of the Se San River. They were stretched out over more than three klicks (kilometers) of shoreline. The river at this time was in high flood.

"This looks like a lure," Williams said to an assistant. "And it's on a wide front. They hope, or expect, we will take these boats and cross over. The ambushes will be ready."

If that was true, the trick didn't work; the water was so high and the current so swift that Parmly ordered his men not to think of crossing. Besides, when a second patrol went forth, it couldn't find the small craft reported to Williams. As the days passed, the monitoring of radio traffic indicated that there could be an enemy force of regimental size somewhere northwest of the Pleijerang camp. Air patrols continued to search the Plei Trap Valley through the daylight hours. They saw nothing to confirm what the electronic sensings said— that the enemy was present in numbers.

Parmly and his men had no choppers in which to hop about at will in the sort of grasshopper existence familiar to the fighting line in those parts. Elements of the Fourth Division, however, displacing easily enough from home base in Pleiku, flew westward to deploy north of Highway No. 19, just in case the enemy was ready to jump at the Pleijerang camp. In so doing, they impelled a local reaction. On 14, 15, and 16 October, one company of Montagnards' (called Yards) moved east, searching out the mountains southeast of the Se San River. It is a kind of nothing country, its only prominent feature being vast reaches of emptiness. In command of the Yards, or rather serving as their chief adviser, was 2nd Lt. Richard E. Dunn, backed up by

S.Sgt. James R. Golding, both of Special Forces. This was not exactly a precautionary move. Dunn, like Parmly who sent him forth, was convinced that the NVA had no intention of attacking the Pleijerang base camp, a view in which they continued to differ with high commands eyeing the same situation. Dunn moved out simply to hunt game.

By the night of the second day the lieutenant was certain he was hot on the trail of an NVA battalion. Approximately seven miles to the south, First Battalion of the 14th U.S. Infantry was in perimeter. Getting the hot message from Dunn, Parmly asked that the battalion be committed as a reaction force, should the company of Yards get in too deep. So far, his men were simply sparring with the outguards of an enemy force, seemingly trying to avoid battle. But it was not play acting: there were frequent brushes, and Golding was knocked out with a chest wound and seven of the Yards were hit by bullets. For the next 36 hours, Dunn's men shadowed the NVA force, all the time asking help from higher command. It did no good; 1/14th wouldn't budge. The decision was made by General Walker, who had his good reasons. Walker was required to protect Pleiku, and he figured he could not let Parmly have the battalion for a reaction force without dropping his guard too low. But that consideration did not ease Parmly's pain one bit; he brooded over what he thought was a lost opportunity and finally withdrew Dunn's company.

Within three days the First of the 14th was lifted to the same ground where Dunn had broken contact. Not surprisingly, it found the birds flown, and all its searching produced naught but wear-and-tear. Artillery had been called in to comfort the nocturnal perimeters; its only effect was disfiguration of the countryside. It seemed to be a land in which nothing moved abroad.

On 6 November, something of a turning point was reached. Maj. Gen. Arthur Collins called a full-dress conference at a halfway station labeled LZ Three Golf. Parmly went to the landing zone arm-in-arm with Colonel Phouc, the bouncy bantam commanding the Kontum Special Military District. Collins outlined the opportunity and response as he saw them. The thing to do was purge the countryside of all enemy forces from the Se San River on the east and south and the Nan Sathay River on the west. Most of this was tough hill country. To mop it thoroughly, he would have to employ at least five battalions sweeping abreast while moving north-northwest. The trouble was that he had enough people to man the sweep, but not enough additional troops to serve as a dustpan.

Collins asked Phouc, "Can you help out with a blocking force?"

Phouc promptly volunteered to commit Parmly's three C.I.D.G. companies, which Parmly, not having been consulted, thought was damned generous of him. In fact, Parmly didn't like any part of the arrangement.

"If we are going to block with my Yards," he told Collins, "then we had better do it in the low ground. As now set, the advance of the five battalions is unprotected on the far flank and rear. The extreme boundary of the battalion farthest west splits the Plei Trap Valley; that makes it congruent with a main infiltration route. All enemy forces in front of you could quickly shift westward and escape to bases in Cambodia."

Collins, having listened carefully, replied, "My orders do not permit me to operate west of the Nan Sathay."

"I understand that quite well," Parmly said, "but we'll be glad to screen for you on the left and rear and at the same time operate as a search-and-destroy force."

Collins agreed with alacrity. He was getting just what the doctor ordered.

"I'll have a task force of the three C.I.D.G. companies ready to go early on 8 November," Parmly continued. "We will maneuver over an area eight klicks wide by sixteen long, north to south, between the Nan Sathay and the Cambodian border. Just have the chopper lift ready to take us out."

It all made sense to Collins, and at that point the conference broke up.

Following it, Parmly made a quick but limited reshuffle of forces within his small but strangely mixed command, some of it Vietnamese, the rest Montagnard with several tribes represented, all of it spiced with U.S. officers or Special Forces NCO's. He knew that one company had superior fighting quality, that a second was at best average, and that the fiber of the third was rated more unknown than dubious. His task of screening necessitated that they operate rather widely separated from one another, and he weighed the likely hazards and forfeits in each area before rebalancing the whole and making his assignments. Two-thirds of the ground to be covered in the northern Plei Trap would go to the 3rd Mike Force Company, his best unit, under Lt. Frank C. Jacobelli. The Pleijerang Company, under Sgt. Carlos D. Caro, would work over the rest of the northern end of the valley. A small AO (area of operations) along the extreme west of the Plei Trap would be given the company from Du Co, under Sgt. 1st Cl. James L. Lewis Jr. The Command Group out of the Special Forces detachment at Pleiku, which would include Parmly, a forward air controller, a radio relay team, an artillery observer, and liaison personnel, would ride along with the Du Co Company. For one small flock of mountain men, this was an unheard-of array of VIP file-closers.

The plans had to be approved by General Collins; Brig. Gen. Dick Lee, the chief U.S. adviser to Lt. Gen. Vinh Loc in Kontum; Col. Judson Miller, commanding the Second Brigade of the Fourth Division, now in operational control of Parmly's companies, and possibly other command levels. It is a complex business, managing a war in tandem. At the same time, the Third Battalion of the 35th Infantry became attached to the Fourth Division. Parmly knew then that the cost of poker was going up. But he still doubted. He expected no quick contact in the Plei Trap. The companies would scout about for 10 days and then be lifted out.

On 8 November, with the first lift getting airborne in Hueys, the ubiquitous copters, at 1000 hours, Parmly's troops moved into the Plei Trap in three waves. Fourth Division had sent a rifle company from 2/8th Infantry to secure a landing zone several hours earlier. First in, the Mike Force Company moved out at once to recon two small hills to the northwest before marching on in that same direction. At 1040 the Pleijerang Company landed and relieved the men of the 8th Infantry guarding the LZ. By 1130 the force from Du Co had set down, routinely and unscratched.

The noon quiet was broken at 1303. The Mike Company, barging on, was already three klicks to the north. Breaking trail for it were Capt. Clyde Sincere and Lieutenant Jacobelli. Their way led through a narrow vale between two smallish, jungle-clad hills. Rounding a turn in the trail, they saw, not 30 meters off, the tail of a North Vietnamese Army antiaircraft battery, the column moving north, its rearward groups manhandling two 12.7 guns. The two officers opened fire and then ran on. The Yards spread into line behind them and came charging. The enemy fled the field, dropping the two heavy guns, five AK-47 rifles, 35 rucksacks, and one dead. It was not quite a bloodless triumph; Jake Jacobelli had taken a bullet through the wrist. Parmly began to change his mind.

The other companies, departing LZ Lane promptly, got only 600 meters to the west and there ran into a "speed trail," a spacious, well-beaten track through jungle, obviously cleared to facilitate rapid military movement. Within the hour, the Pleijerang Company, scouting this avenue to the west, ran into a three-man NVA carrying party and wiped it out. It got no credit.

Parmly heard the news and told it over his radio telephone, "You're going the wrong way; change direction and get into your proper AO." He continued to march west with the column from Du Co.

However, by nightfall, when all units went on the defensive, nothing new had been added to the score. Even so, Parmly no longer blew cold. By 1615 the Pleijerang Company had emerged onto a clearing, run into another party of NVA, fired, missed, then engaged in futile pursuit. What impressed him more, however, was that prepared, unmanned enemy positions were almost as ubiquitous as were the anthills.

At 0805 next morning Parmly got a message over the RT from the Pleijerang Company: "We are in contact with the security elements of an NVA battalion. We collided with it going south along the trail. We are firing. They are now crossing a stream."

Five minutes later the company reported, "Now we are stopped by heavy fire from the south bank."

Still later came the word: "We assaulted across the stream, but were driven back."

Parmly put in a hurry call for tac (tactical air support)

strikes. A 105-mm. battery from the Fourth Division was in place on yet another landing zone about five klicks east of the fighting ground. Having already been given the coordinates, Parmly called for supporting fire. The fight droned on through the morning, but Parmly, at that distance, could get little impression of it, which chafed him more, though he continued to cool his heels.

In mid-afternoon a message came from the Pleijerang Company: "We need help! Our casualties are moderate. But all leaders are dead or wounded. That means Caro is hit, also Specialist 4 David Quigley. The Yard commander is out of action; so are four squad leaders and three platoon leaders. And I think we are being surrounded."

That's when Parmly, his Command Group, and the Du Co Company got moving; they made the four kilometers of rough trail in less than an hour. By 1600, under the covering fire provided by a catch-as-catch-can skirmish line formed more out of rank than by file, the embattled company had broken free, withdrawing with four Montagnards dead and 15 wounded. From that point, it was another hard march back to LZ Lane again so that the casualties could be evacuated. There was little else to show for it—a count of four enemy KIA and one machine gun captured. The luck was all still with the Mike Force Company. While clearing another LZ that day five klicks north of LZ Lane, so that Hueys could get in to move the AA guns back as prizes, it had bushwhacked an NVA squad, killing four, wounding four others. On 10 November, while marching north toward a salt flat called Bay Ho Lake, it had repeated this trick, killing four and capturing three men already wounded. On arriving at Bay Ho, it wiped out a few snipers, still with no one getting hit. Sincere had called in a Huey to take the several POW's back to Pleiku for interrogation under his escort. (Special Forces had their own pet name for the salt flat, calling it Pali Wali Lake.)

The 10th was also a big day for powwowing. Collins, Walker, and Miller flew out to LZ Lane, where Parmly met them at 0910. Landing at the same time was C/1/14th, under Capt. Charline Federline (his was a name from the Indian wars), who truly didn't belong there. Federline's left arm was in a cast, having been broken just a few hours before in a Huey crash at Pleiku. Some hours later Federline would be killed in action.

"My feeling," Parmly said to Collins and the others, "is that yesterday my one company fighting along the stream was bumping one sector of a well-fortified line; the place is just about one mile north of the Cambodian border."

His troops, he continued, had nowhere run into anything larger than an enemy company. But the presence of the AA guns argued that there might be several battalions present. A prisoner of war had said the troops around Bay Ho Lake were from the 88th Regiment. The banks of the creeks, where the one good fight had taken place, were scarred with freshly turned works. By nature, it was also formidably fixed—double-canopy country, covered densely by brush, with heavy bamboo tangles and thorn copses.

Collins and Miller talked it over; their decision was to go after the fortified line. Federline's company would strike directly south from LZ Lane to hit the position from the east flank.

Collins asked Parmly, "Can your people then move south along the trail and pin them from the front so that Charley Company can roll them up?"

"I am sure that by now they will be waiting for us on the trail," Parmly replied, "but I think that with 185 men I ought to be able to take them.''

One may idly wonder if a realist's view of tactical circumstance conditioned these judgments. Parmly, the only one who had seen the ground, might have urged more caution. Or having a real go at it with all possible heavy weapons might have been weighed as a more promising option. Most likely, in these circumstances, all command levels react too strongly, like beagles scenting game. The evidence of the senses takes over, leaving little choice in the matter. So the scenario becomes akin to that encountered when a gent on a subway train sees some carefree drunk pinch his wife's bottom. This is not to suggest that they felt an upsurge of gallantry about it.

Parmly at this time had at least one strong conviction; he wanted no more fighting operations for his Yards unless there was a U.S. unit somewhere near. He knew that, in a very real sense, his units were being used as bait; that part of it was all right, a logical role for an irregular force. But if the companies were to be used for fixing and holding rather than screening, he wanted dependable relief close by. Anyhow, by now he was well in it.

At 1100 Federline's company moved out.

Having prepared his order, Parmly gathered the Yard leaders and the Americans together and read them a small lecture on terrain, tactics, and traps.

"If you remember," he said, "we have three danger spots along this trail. The first is the spot 500 meters from here where we crossed the stream over the log bridge. The second is that cleared area where the Pleijerang Company sighted the three NVA and smelled the dead bodies. The third is the stream where we fought yesterday. Don't rush any of these places. Take it slow and easy.''

By 1150 the column was lined up and ready, pointed

south; and, at that moment, its tail was sprayed with fire by an NVA squad that, undetected, had closed to within easy range from the north. Two Montagnards were shot down; everybody hit the dirt. One NVA soldier was killed before the enemy squad could wiggle away.

Parmly thought out loud, "They figured we were about to extract. They came to give us a few parting shots. But since we are not going, and the odds are so heavily against them, they fired anyway to send along the word that we are coming."

Whether this was inspired reasoning, it prompted Parmly to stay the march-out until the on-call artillery could work over his three danger spots, which doubtless was more comfort to him than discomfort to the NVA. A 105-mm. howitzer, firing at a jungle mass, is somewhat deadlier than a peashooter, though not much. When the column, dubbed Task Force Prong, at last marched, Parmly was looking over his shoulder. He knew that LZ Lane was the all-important terrain feature. There was not another piece of ground in the Plei Trap to put down troops in any number.

The column spread out as its point came to each of the danger spots. Sgt. Jerry T. Wyatt of the Du Co crowd was in charge of right-flank security. Caro, being wounded, stayed with the main body, though his company did the outguarding on the left.

At the first stream, when danger did not materialize, Parmly sat on the log bridge during the halt, talking to Spec. 4 John E. Mitchell, an acting sergeant. Mitchell was a short-timer with 32 days to go before return to the United States. He was showing Parmly a snapshot of his two children.

"Why did you come on this operation when you could have ducked it?" Parmly asked.

Mitchell considered, then replied matter-of-factly, "I have been spending too much time sitting on my can in bunkers. Before I go, I want to see at least one show." He said it in a simple, unemphatic way, and, at the time, what he said impressed no one, though he was voicing the natural curiosity of the average good infantry fighter. Hours later, men repeated those words of his as if they were pearls.

"I know what you mean," Parmly said. "You'd never be happy with yourself if you missed out on that one thing. It's why I came along." Parmly had a great liking for Mitchell, unalloyed by any worry that Mitchell was pushing his luck. They talked on for several minutes.

Then they marched on. At 1400 hours the head of the column moved slowly, cautiously, onto the edge of the cleared area, about which Parmly had warned all hands before the jumpoff. Now that he saw it under full sunlight, the clearing, twice the size of a baseball diamond, looked anything but ominous. The trail led straight through the brightened center. Though the trees did not arch far enough to close out the light, three-fourths of the clearing was in deep shade. The Du Co outfit was holding to the trail, well forward, where it was supposed to be. The Pleijerang force, which had been told to come up on a parallel to the left on reaching the clearing, was dragging its feet, too far to the rear. Parmly, angered by its hesitation, dashed that way to pull the flank forward. He grabbed the Montagnard serving as first scout by the shirt to hustle him along.

In the same moment, an NVA soldier stood in the open, 30 meters to the front, right at the edge of the clearing. There can be little doubt about the role of this soldier. He was a live decoy, put there at the risk of his

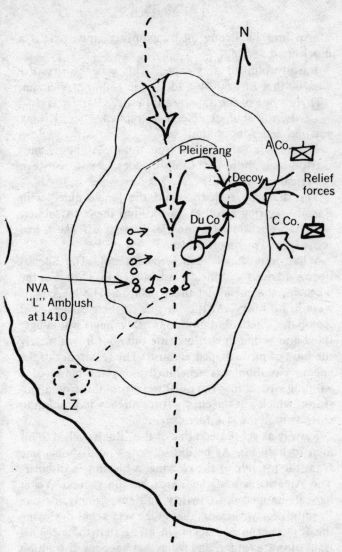

U.S. attack that led to ambush of TF Prong. Enemy formed
L-shaped block across path. Arrows show U.S. units heading
into trap. Decoy lured outfits to east.

life to lure TF Prong on by exposing himself. It is a much-used device.

Parmly blinked and gaped. This was the first live Charlie that Eleazar IV had seen in action in Vietnam. "There's one of them, Sergeant Lewis," Parmly said.

Lewis, the soul of deference, replied, "Sir, I think you had better shoot him."

It sounds too stilted to be true. But the Alphonse-and-Gaston act, however foolish, does persist between Americans in uniform.

The dialogue ended, as did the jungle quiet, with Parmly pouring a full M-16 clip into the NVA soldier, who had not moved a muscle. It went off like a bad scene from a mediocre tableau.

What immediately followed did not. The Special Forces advisers and their Yards surged forward. For the moment, the enemy let them rush on. The NVA units were in no hurry. At the far side of the clearing, First Company, Sixth Battalion, 33rd Regiment, was snugly fixed and prone in shallow rifle pits, but it was merely the base of an L-shaped ambush. The remainder of the enemy battalion was echeloned along the banks of a winding stream that ran northwest from this frontal position, which put the enemy force already in position to close around the task force's rear.

Parmly as yet sensed none of this. But he yelled to his men to hold up. As he did so, a few wild shots came from the far side of the clearing, a blessing in disguise. The Americans and the Yards hit the ground. Yet it had all happened so swiftly and surprisingly, despite Parmly's early warning, that in the very act of deploying the force began to buckle. In going flat, the men lost sight of one another, and when that happens dissolution begins and control erodes rapidly.

Parmly's first thoughts were: "I've been lucky so far, but I must get people moving." Most of the Americans, and some of the Yards, on going flat, had opened fire. Their initial shots were enough to bring the Charlies out of their holes to join the action. Bullets from 10 or more automatic weapons were now mowing the elephant grass on both sides of the trail. The Command Group men were still strung out along that pathway, some flat, some kneeling, according to how the ground lay. The communicators were also scattered along this line.

Not bothering about that for the moment, Parmly said to Capt. Robert H. Berry, his operations officer, "Take the Pleijerang Company, hook wide to the left, away from the clearing, and try to get on the enemy flank." Berry took off promptly with the unit. Parmly figured he could lose nothing by such a move. Should Berry not succeed in finding a dangling flank, he would in any case form a block between the North Vietnamese and LZ Lane, directly northeast of the enemy line.

Momentarily, Parmly got another bonus from it. Berry's maneuver drew off the enemy fire and the clearing began to cool a bit. As the pressure eased off, the Command Group picked up and resumed the movement forward—seven U.S. Special Forces hot shots and seven other U.S. service attachments, all guarded, so to speak, by one platoon from the Du Co Company, which had a light machine gun. The rest of Du Co Company was beyond accounting for; about 35 of them had bugged out for the landing zone, others had suddenly become students of nature and the science of playing it safe. Parmly did not yet know this. Seeing the small numbers, he mistakenly thought the enemy fire had killed a large part of his command.

Berry and the Pleijerang men, detached for other

reasons, got 120 meters to east of the trail, where they ran into heavy automatic fire from the front while a machine gun nipped their tails from the rear. Thus wedged, they flattened. Berry could see what was happening: both sides were extending simultaneously to the east, each probing for the other's open flank. But the gun on his rear was his main concern; it meant that Charlie was already between him and LZ Lane. The advance of the Du Co men had been halted by Parmly at the far edge of the clearing. He told the Command Group to "form a tight perimeter of Americans only" at the head of the column while he worked things out. Then he called that ubiquitous gunner, Lieutenant "Fearless" Fosdick, to tell him, "For God's sake, get ready to pour the fire on ahead of us." Parmly suddenly corrected himself. "Put it on all sides of us," he said. Fosdick already had the coordinates for the shot.

Parmly was bothered at the disappearance of the once by tac ships strafing with mixed loads—argued that they had fallen back to a stronger position. As he signed off after calling Fosdick, a better idea hit him. He would move all the rest of the TF east and link up with Berry. He yelled out so that all hands would hear him: "Let's get the hell off of this trail!" It was done on the impulse of the moment.

As he yelled, Parmly jumped off the trail and into the bush, a move made just a split second late. A heavy machine gun fired from 50 or so meters uptrail. Spec. 4 Francis E. Simmons, carrying the top-heavy PRC-74 radio on his back, took a bullet in his left thigh and screamed like a panther; the slug had shattered his thigh bone. Acting Sergeant Mitchell, weighted with the PRC-25, was drilled through the left shoulder. Maj. Charles W. Buttermore took a bullet in the left foot and hit the ground hard. These things shook Parmly.

He yelled to Lt. Michael Lapolla, the attached liaison officer, "Call Gil Proctor! Have him divert Charley Company this way. Tell him we're fighting a lot of people." Lapolla made the call, only to be shaken off, Proctor telling him, "Nothing doing, I'm holding to my plan."

"Can I talk to the brigade commander?" Lapolla asked.

Proctor replied, "Permission denied."

The lieutenant—for the moment, the man in the middle—made his own decision. Without asking Parmly, he went over Proctor's head.

Jud Miller welcomed the call, telling Lapolla, "You'll get Charley Company and beyond that—I'll send Alpha along and get it into the fight."

The news hardly soothed Parmly; until he saw more troops arrive, he told himself, he'd have not one good minute.

From somewhere aloft, an FAC pilot suddenly came in on Parmly's freak (frequency) and identified himself: "I'm Captain Partridge."

Parmly asked, "Do you know Colonel Eugene Dietrich, CO of 1st Air Commando Squadron at Pleiku?"

"Sure do," Partridge replied.

"Good," said Parmly. "Then give him the word that his old classmate is in deep shit down here."

Maybe that could be called working the old school tie till the knot gets frayed. Even so, Parmly got Dietrich's forget-you-not within less than 10 minutes. First, two gunships came over and made their runs with rockets. They were followed at once by tac ships strafing with mixed loads—napalm, general purpose bombs, and CBU's—making 11 sorties altogether. The air attack was laid on from 1330 to 1700. Knowing that the air would stop NVA reaction while it lasted, Parmly used the bombardment as cover to move his people to the east of the trail.

By now he believed that the enemy was in strength on a fairly wide front to his south, with other forces echeloned to the west of the trail for some distance, which put them in position to swing round his rear if he did not move. Most of this was inspired guessing; he had still felt no pressure from the westward.

So, as the tac ships and Puff the Magic Dragon came on to continue the strafing, Parmly radioed, "We are now east of the trail. Keep hitting Charlie about 50 meters west of the trail and all along our front to the south of us."

Men on the extreme flanks of Task Force Prong continued to pop smoke grenades for the attacking aircraft to guide on. Parmly wanted to call for artillery, but with so much traffic overhead he figured that he dared not risk it.

As the force settled in position east of the trail, a heavy machine gun opened fire directly in front of it, serving notice to Parmly that his swing-out to the left had been observed. But he was given no time to worry about that: two grenades came sailing in on the Command Group. The first exploded into an anthill. One frag from it hit Capt. David D. Casto in the back. Another hit Mitchell in the chest. Parmly, straining to locate the machine gun, was hardly aware of the explosion.

Then the second grenade hit and exploded. Parmly felt something sting him in the neck and forehead. "Hey, guy," he called to Casto, "there are bees around here."

He wasn't kidding. He really thought an insect had bit him. Casto took a look at Parmly and grunted, "You damned fool, you've been hit."

Casto stood up to look for the grenadier. As he did so, a Vietnamese arose directly in front of him, arm cocked to throw another grenade. Casto shot him dead at a range of 10 feet.

By mid-afternoon, Captain Berry, 150 meters to the east of where Parmly had become engaged, was able to pull together his part of the task force and get it fighting as a body. He told Parmly over the RT, "We're in pretty good position; we're on a slope with large trees, mainly banyans, giving us protection."

Certain now that the greater number of NVA were disposed to his southwest, Parmly figured that the best thing to do was to pull out and rejoin Berry's force. He himself led off, carrying the PRC-74, a 49-pound load. That was because the radio operator, Simmons, had been critically wounded and was no longer mobile. Parmly first blazed the trail for the others, accompanied only by two Yard strikers. Once in Berry's perimeter, he instructed the Pleijerang men where to lay their covering fire so that the displacement would go as smoothly as possible. Even so, it was an encumbered, halting operation. One Special Forces soldier had been blinded. Two Montagnards had had their eyes shot out, and eight other Yards had received crippling wounds. That reduced the effectives among the incoming force to less than 20 men, with 60 others, or one-third of the body that had set forth from LZ Lane, unaccounted for. Parmly continued to report, "I have taken about 50 percent casualties," still not knowing that most of these losses were runaways.

As the headquarters and Du Co people, winded but otherwise not hurt during the maneuver, closed on Berry's force, machine-gun fire came against the hill from out of the northwest. Parmly knew then that his gloomy forebodings were more than realized. The

enemy had swung wide to the east and was now blocking
the trail. The main question was whether this maneuver
across their rear also closed the direct line to LZ Lane.

The hour was 1620 and there would be about another
90 minutes of useful daylight. Parmly by this time was
sweating out a dilemma—whether his duty was to attempt saving the force through movement or to hold the
line and hope for help. He knew that A/1/14 had
already maneuvered to the south of LZ Lane. But he
wasn't sure where. He finally decided that he'd better
get out of it if he could; he would try moving back to the
landing zone over the trail that the retrograde movement had broken the day before.

"You take one platoon and attack northeast," he
told Caro. "Try to secure a stream crossing somewhere
to the east of where we are now, and let me know. I will
follow with carrying parties assisting the wounded. That
will take every man we've got."

The next bit came harder. Specialist Mitchell, his
radio telephone operator, had already been wounded
twice and was badly shaken. On the other hand, Parmly
still trusted the acting sergeant's judgment more than
that of any other RTO.

"Will you go with Caro and signal me when your feet
touch the bank of the creek about 500 meters from
here?" he asked Mitchell. "Then we'll come along."

Mitchell simply nodded. Most of the enemy fire had
quieted. The platoon under Caro took off. At Parmly's
request, Wyatt had gone along to tote the PRC-74 because Mitchell was too weak to carry anything.

They made 40 meters along the trail; then a storm
of automatic fire came against the platoon front, most
of it going high. One bullet drilled Mitchell through
the chest. Wyatt was hit in the right thumb. The im-

pact spun him around and the weight of the PRC-74 slammed him to the ground, spraining his back. A burst of four bullets hit his radio, destroying it. With that, the platoon recoiled all the way back to the perimeter.

"Where's Mitchell?" Parmly asked.

No one had missed him.

"My God," Caro said, "I didn't know."

Caro rallied a squad, returned to the spot, and brought Mitchell's body out. It had taken 10 minutes. For four of those minutes, under machine-gun fire, Caro had tried mouth-to-mouth resuscitation on Mitchell. It was already too late.

The day was wearing out as dusk took over briefly. Parmly got on the RT to Proctor and told him of their plight.

Proctor said, "I'll send Alpha Company down the trail from the LZ."

"Anywhere but the trail," Parmly warned. "Don't use that trail!"

It was Parmly's first knowledge that Federline's search for the North Vietnamese flank had missed.

Parmly reckoned that it might take another two hours for the relieving force to come through. Beginning at 1900, when it was full dark, he stood with Casto at the northeast corner of the perimeter, after contracting the position severely. Caro and Wyatt stood at the southeast corner. It was just an added safeguard. They wanted to be sure that their Yards didn't fire on the friendly column when it appeared. But there was no fire of any kind after sundown and the relief unit didn't come knocking until well past midnight. That didn't make them less welcome; there was a real doctor among them, the battalion surgeon. His coming gave the force a double uplift.

Parmly talked to the two company commanders, Captains Federline and Boggs. They agreed to wrap another perimeter all the way around the defensive circle held by the Yards, 25 meters out beyond the position. Parmly and the others would sleep well that night, despite the friendly shelling on all four sides of them. Next morning, Parmly, with the Du Co platoon, searched the battlefield. Fifteen enemy bodies were found inside the perimeter that Boggs and Federline had set. Outside of it were found 12 NVA dead and the body of one Du Co soldier. All the dead Charlies were still with their weapons. The patrol also found a flat space suitable for the landing of a dustoff chopper. The casualties were flown out—one U.S. and four Montagnard dead, two U.S. and 19 Montagnard WIA's. The more lightly wounded, such as Parmly, carried on.

Federline's company marched west through the day. Parmly and his men stayed on in a defensive position encircling a new landing zone 600 meters to the southwest of LZ Lane. That night, the force posted ambush parties along several trails outward from the perimeter. Just before midnight an NVA platoon, moving north, bumped into the Yards, who were blocking 400 meters to the south of the perimeter. The blocking party was well fixed, with one heavy machine gun, a crew of three, and 10 riflemen. The machine gunners fired off one box of ammunition, which duty done, the entire patrol fled hastily back to the main position. It was not, as Parmly remarked, a brilliant feat of arms, though he was not unhappy that he had missed it.

At Pali Wali Lake the Mike Company had positioned one 50-man platoon at the northwest corner of the dry salt flat early on the same morning of 11 November. No one marked the calendar or said, "This is Veterans' Day." The main body was in a foxholed circular defen-

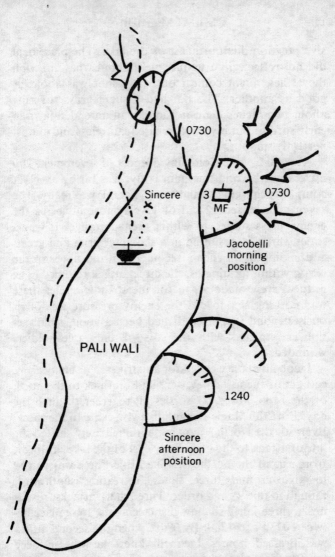

0730

0730

Sincere

3
MF

Jacobelli
morning
position

PALI WALI

1240

Sincere
afternoon
position

Fight at Pali Wali Lake, the salt flat, showing position of
Mike Force (MF). Sincere, dropping from chopper, took command once Jacobelli was wounded.

sive position due northeast of the lake. The placement did not reflect any true judgment about what direction the attack might come from. One spot was about as good as another. The flat had a slight grass covering about two inches high, not unlike an untended lawn in early spring. But it was otherwise featureless and almost perfectly smooth.

At 0600 a Mike Company outpost of seven men, 200 meters out beyond the main body, was hit by an NVA company, charging straight on. That OP was ready. The seven men loosed 12 out of 15 claymore mines as the enemy mass surged to within grenade range. It was a shock surprise, resulting in a slaughter grim and great, and ending in an enemy recoil. But it did not stop the NVA; within 15 minutes, the direct attack resumed. The outpost crew made a run for the foxhole circle: there was nothing else to do; the enemy pressure was obviously beyond its power. It had been a good, small action, completed with the loss of only one soldier, wounded.

Jacobelli at once called for air strikes, "as many as we can get of them." They were laid on thick to the north of the Mike Force, 27 sorties all together through the day. Puff the Magic Dragon likewise came to the show. Even so, the North Vietnamese immediately shifted the line of attack to the main body east of the lake, hitting it from out of the northeast. The Mike Force was forced to give ground three times, retreating southward, though in fairly good order. Three sharp attacks, resulting in three fairly shallow displacements, took place between 0730 and 1240. By 0900, when the second attack was pressed home, Jacobelli knew he was in deep trouble from more than one direction.

He reported to Parmly over the RT, "I am taking heavy casualties, as much as one-third of my force."

Fretting him almost as much was the fact that his men were running short of ammunition.

Captain Sincere, after he had finished working over the several NVA POW's at Pleiku, had hitchhiked a ride that morning aboard an ammo-loaded Huey bound for Pali Wali Lake. With him was Lt. Paul J. Hess, a quartermaster officer, who came along out of curiosity. Their ship hove in sight just as Jacobelli was having his worst sweat, which coincided with a brief break in the action.

Jacobelli, speaking over the radio, said, "Bring that ammo down and do it right now."

Just then things went wrong because of a few words left unsaid. Sincere, on leaving the company the day before, had been lifted from west of the lake. He assumed the Mike Force was still there. So before Jacobelli had time to understand what was happening, the Huey was in a steep glide to the far side of the salt flat while Jake and his men were crying for ammunition 200 meters to the east, the flat being about 150 meters wide.

When only a few feet above earth, the pilot guessed that something was wrong, braked the descent, and turned to ask a question on the intercom. As the Huey hovered, Sincere jumped free, thinking that this was what was wanted. From the edge of the woods, 50 meters away, a machine gun opened fire. The first burst killed Hess and the crew chief, Spec. 5 John Leonard. As they crumpled within the machine, the Huey bounced high and was soon winging away from the scene, leaving Sincere stranded.

Sincere was now drawing fire from two sides. Still thinking that the Mike Force was on his side of the lake, he bolted toward where he had left his men, running straight toward the enemy. Some kind of projectile hit him. It glanced off his webbed gear just above the heart without exploding but knocked him flat. It had not broken skin; he was unhurt. In the moment that he lay there, trying to catch breath, Sincere saw a dozen enemy soldiers break from the woods and run toward him. He realized his only chance for life was to lay perfectly still and feign death should they come all the way. Curiosity, however, did not take them that far; the will to live restrained them. They turned back at the halfway point, and Sincere lay there for hours. Part of the deterrent was that Mike Force, from east of the lake, had witnessed his plight and was giving it to these Charlies with all weapons.

Jacobelli's line was again under direct attack by 1000, though the NVA came on more feebly in an action that was finally broken off at 1240. Colonel Miller, in the meantime, had committed an element of the 4th Infantry Division to relieve Mike Force. Although Sincere, who had safely made it to the company during the noon hour, advised that the lake was now safe for a landing, the main body of the relieving battalion put down in a landing zone almost two miles northeast of Mike Force. Bravo Company and one battery of artillery were set down right in the middle of the salt flat.

Sincere had taken command. Jacobelli was down from a bullet wound in the abdomen that later cost him a kidney. Sgt. Frank C. Huff had taken a bullet in the left foot; Sgt. Francis Quinn was wounded in the left arm.

Before the fight sputtered out, Parmly had flown in on a Huey to see how Mike Force was faring. It was not too good. Of its Montagnard fighters, 13 were dead and 41 had been wounded in action; U.S. casualties were as previously noted. During the policing of the field that quickly followed, 58 NVA bodies were counted, indicating an enemy loss in excess of 200. So it had to have been a battalion that had attacked.

Parmly rolled one dead captain from Fifth Battalion, 88th NVA Regiment. In his pack he found a Christmas present from the captain's wife, a ballpoint pen and pencil set under the brand name of "Hero." Parmly said laconically to Sincere, "My conscience permits me to accept this as a Christmas present from another man's wife, since he can't use it, and I am a hero of sorts."

Parmly, at this point, was feeling better than he had for several days. He thought his own TF was probably well out of it and that the fighting in the Plei Trap was through, at least for this one go-round. But even as a small wave may reshape sand on a beach, Task Force Prong's limited adventure had not done more than merely indicate from which direction the tide was moving. There were heavier rollers to come, which is the way things go in fighting along the Cambodian border.

The Pali————————————
————————————Wali Doodle

By the night of 10 November, Lieutenant Colonel
Parmly had realized that his men were in heavy trouble
and would not beat back from it under their own power.
It was time to signal an SOS.

The rescue mission was given First Battalion of the
12th Infantry Regiment (4th Division) long after dark
and too late to do anything about it that night except
fret.

Parmly had not understated the plight. By his ac-
count, the C.I.D.G. company trapped near the dry salt
flat that Special Forces called Pali Wali Lake (coordinates 572-555) had been cut off for two days, losing 40
percent of its strength while killing 58 of the enemy.
"They can't hold out another hour," he said. Events
proved his estimate to be a somewhat pardonable exaggeration.

When the call got through to Lt. Col. James R. Lay,
the CO, his battalion was anything but collected. Bravo
Company, the Batallion Reconnaissance Platoon, the
4.2 Mortar Platoon, and one battery of artillery
(B/4/42) were well established on one landing zone
northwest of Pleijerang. (This position was at 71-7535.)

118

Charley Company was in perimeter 3,000 meters to the northeast on a one-ship landing zone. Alpha Company was based on yet another LZ in the opposite direction.

So it was arranged that Bravo Company would move out as the relieving force in the Pali Wali business. Alpha Company would stand steady in reserve, waiting to see what developed. The artillery battery would be lifted and shifted to ground 2,200 meters east of the Cambodian border, whence, at a range of about five miles from the beleaguered force, it could provide fire support. Charley Company and the other lesser elements would head the same way and establish a perimeter to secure the battery.

The guns were under the command of Capt. Harold B. Flody Jr., 26, of Cumberland, R.I., a graduate of Providence College. Flody is a very intense soldier, almost painfully solemn and professional, but quick on the uptake. Charley Company was under Lt. James E. Bigelow II, USMA '64, a Vermonter.

Next morning, time really wasted. Due to communications trouble, orders were slow in getting to the forces on the big LZ. When at last they came, the attendant pressure was immoderate. "Get ready to move right now," Captain Freeman, the batallion S-3, ordered. "You're first on a combat assault." The roar of the arriving liftships was already over them. So it was rush, rush at LZ Warrior. (The battalion calls itself the Red Warriors.) Bigelow was in such a hurry that he did not gather his platoon commanders together to spell out the mission. They took off still not knowing where they were going.

Bigelow was airborne in the first Huey. Flody followed on the second. Both minds were set on reconnoitering the landing zone before the troops came on. On their way, as they circled to come in for a landing,

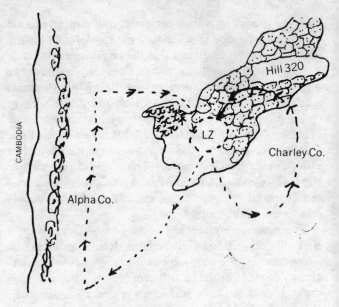

The movements of the two patrols, Alpha and Charley Companies, close to Cambodian border.

they saw a chopper down and burning one-half mile west of the designated ground. Flody said to Bigelow over the radio, "It looks like we got problems."

When they touched earth it was just about high noon. Within a few minutes the big Chinooks came in sight, bringing Charley Company and members of the battery. It became a mean little scramble, as the emergency was truly not that great.

Some of the choppers would not put down; to be blunt about it, the pilots were rattled. Lt. David R. Dresia, 25, of San Rafael, a U. of California grad, had to jump 10 or so feet combat-loaded (he estimated it at "15 feet") while the Chinook hovered. He landed badly shaken and felt sore as hell about it. Afterwards he hobbled about on a sprained ankle, as did two of his RTO's. It was already a battered, bruised outfit. More than half of the troops made this leap through space over distances higher than a man's head. The chopper pilots had done an execrable job.

There was no time to cry about that. Flody, already pressing, asked Bigelow, "Where will you place your perimeter?" Bigelow was fretting about picking the spots for his howitzers. Bigelow made a sweep of his arm, indicating the area. Within a stone's throw was a rough oval of higher ground, too low to be worth one contour on the map, but still good enough to lift the weapons above the field over which they would fire. It measured about 125 meters north to south by 75 meters east to west, which was suitable, because they reckoned the main threat would come from the west. This gradually sloping rise was densely grown with cane and elephant grass, the stand averaging better than head-high.

The riflemen starting digging the moment they deployed. The ground was quite soft. So close that they could hardly keep their eyes on their work was the blazing Huey. Specialist 4 Carey said, "Look at that long enough and you'll want to dig deep."

One other thing goaded them. As Pfc. Michael E. Reilly, 21, of New York City plied his spade, a bullet came out of nowhere and creased his forehead, barely breaking the skin. Having missed death by an inch, Reilly kept right on digging, not bothering to yell for an aid man. He simply continued to mop his head with a handkerchief.

S.Sgt. John E. Potteiger of Harrisburg, Pa., and Spec. 4 William L. Sensenbach had no need to dig. They found a ready-made hole and settled into it. The hole was waist-deep with straight walls.

"This looks like an AA position," Potteiger said.

"That means the NVA has used this ground," Sensenbach remarked, "and knows right where we are."

They set up their M-60 machine guns on the berm, facing west.

Flody didn't have time to witness the setting of even his first howitzer before discovering that this would be no picnic ground. As he started to move out a mortar shell exploded 15 feet behind his back. Fortunately, the round blew out westward or he would have died. Flody merely wondered what the loud bang meant and later felt stupid that he had not known. This was his first time under fire.

Despite these interruptions, the corporate effect continued untroubled. The men had no proportioned feeling about one anonymous bullet and a shell that had hurt no one. They did not jump for cover; there was no excited talk. Everything was too new and too sudden, and the day was quite hot.

Their first impression of the landscape had been its emptiness. The air is beautifully clear in this region when the monsoon is not on, and, though South Vietnam is almost everywhere a country of magnificent distances, here the land seems to stretch endlessly. The earth rolls out, billow after billow of fertile hill, swale and dale, never trod by a buffalo or turned for planting. The few huts where people live, or once did, are leagues apart. There are no burned-out, half-cleared patches on the slopes. Bamboo, followed by forest patches, giving way to meadow and farther on a stretch of scrub, more bamboo—it is all like that. The verdure covering one small row of hills may have every shade of green. It is a landscape simplified, going on and on, subtle, yet nigh featureless under the breathtaking vastness of the sky.

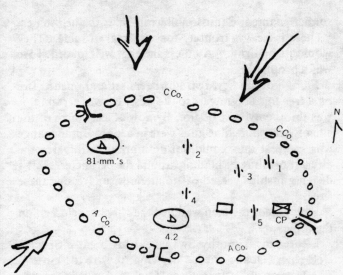

U.S. perimeter with gun sites and the defensive setup that came under enemy attack.

Bigelow called the battalion commander, who was several miles distant and airborne in a Chinook, and told him about the mortar round. It had taken Flody five minutes to learn what the big bang was about and he felt a little sheepish. But not for long. His first howitzer was just setting down and, coincidental with its arrival, he heard the beat-and-bark of a machine gun off to the west. The air above them throbbed with motors and rotors. An armada of aircraft—slicks bearing gun crews, Chinooks with the heavy stuff and still more troops, gunships to protect them and scout about —were all coming at once.

That first enemy machine gun—a heavy on wheels— still fired. It was about 700 meters to the west. A young soldier named Santos Villareal said to his mates, "There's heavy trouble for us—real trouble. They wouldn't be firing AA unless they are well loaded." He was a prophet.

Flody got his first two howitzers set and opened fire on a tree line 600 meters to the west. He was certain this was the enemy base of fire. By now at least three of the enemy heavy machine guns were in action. But the range was so great they could not do more than threaten the aircraft orbiting or landing around the perimeter. Half a dozen gunships veered off to attempt suppressing these fires.

Fascinated, the men watched the choppers close in on the target area.

Lieutenant Timothy Swan held his breath. Spec. 4 Delbert A. Doane cried, "My God, they're too close!" The 21-year-old from Eugene, Ore., had called the turn.

Rockets rose from the wood patch like a Roman candle, crossing the streams of tracers. Eight hundred meters to the west a gunship went into a slow, unspectacular glide to the north, hit the ground, and burst into a ball of flame. Then another was hit, and they watched the fall, but did not see it burn. One Huey that had come in bearing some of Flody's men had taken off on the same course as the gunships. It, too, was shot down. These things had happened within the span of a few minutes. The three ships had gone down as evenly as ducks passing a marksman in a carnival shooting gallery. The wrecks were distributed quite neatly on a line 800 meters from the base camp.

The troops around Flody and Dresia beheld the spectacle as if transfixed, for the moment speechless, their mouths open in startled disbelief. Being witness to any air tragedy in Vietnam is as great a shock to today's soldier as was the sight of a friendly sausage balloon being gunned down in flames to the doughboy with Pershing. Men never get used to it.

The troops resumed digging, spading furiously. Within an hour the position was fairly well rounded out. Flody had only 20 rounds on hand for the opening blast at the tree line with the howitzers, and so he couldn't give it much of a go. But the 4.2- and 81-mm. mortars had also set up and were working over the target area. (There were four 4.2 tubes and as many 81's, with 600 rounds between them.) The infantry armament otherwise seemed to be sufficient for whatever might come. Riflemen averaged 400 rounds for their M-16's and carried two frag and two smoke grenades apiece, with six claymore mines per squad. With each M-60 machine gun were 1,200 rounds, the standard load. The M-79 grenadiers were set with about 60 rounds apiece.

Westward, the roar and racket built up steadily. Air strikes—jets and 81-E's—were now hammering the wood line with napalm, bombs, rockets, and CBU's. One section of the forest was ablaze. Flody still had no notion whether there had been a real force in there or just a few AA gun crews, but he doubted that anyone by now could be left alive.

So passed another hour, ending with another shock. A crewman from one of the wrecked Hueys stumbled into their position. He was burned black from crown to toe. In a strangled tone, he cried feebly, "Help, help, help."

They rushed to him.

The crewman got only a few more words out, gasping between each one of them, "I—walked—five—miles—to—get—here." Then he pitched over face forward, and shortly after that he died. Flody had asked him one question, "What happened to the others?" There was no reply; he seemed not to have heard.

At 1400 the men got the word that Mike Force at Pali Wali Lake had been succored. Resupply Hueys had flown into the position just before noon, orbited above it and received no fire, and therefore set down. Of this test came the first awareness that the enemy had moved elsewhere. Bravo Company headed directly into Pali Wali, closing at 1430. Other ships then moved in to lift out the troops. This is the form in which the story got to Flody, Doane, and the others. So at least that part of their mission had been accomplished. The reflection gave them a moment of sober satisfaction.

All along they had been wondering what was happening to Alpha Company, and they were hoping that its troops would shortly reappear. As things stood, the perimeter was only half-manned. Besides, they would get some comfort from it, misery loving company.

Alpha Company had gone through a restful day, accomplishing virtually nothing. At the Pali Wali position, Bravo Company did a little better. Lt. Tom Jones, a Syracuse University man commanding First Platoon, set a six-man ambush along a trail outside the perimeter (coordinates 572-544). Four NVA soldiers walked into it. One was killed and the others got away whole-skinned, a not unusual score.

For Charley Company, the remainder of the afternoon slipped away uneventfully. Alpha Company was lifted into the position at 1745 and set about digging its foxhole line facing east. The night was not exactly quiet. The Chinooks had brought in 1,500 rounds of high explosive and 200 rounds of white phosphorous and illumination for Flody's five howitzers. A resupply of 250 rounds had also come in for the 4.2 mortars. When ammo is plentiful, gunners will fire it. So through the night there was a continual blasting of the wood line and some use of harassing rounds in other directions. Except for the shooting, which rarely disturbs a rifleman's dreams, the next 12 hours passed serenely.

Starting at 0730 next morning, 12 November, Charley Company made a march that did a full circle of the perimeter, one-half mile out. Enroute they picked up one POW, so ill with malaria that, too feeble to unbutton his trousers, he stank of his own excrement. The maneuver took them in due course to the much-battered wood line. Beyond it they found little or nothing—some rations scattered about, blood trails here and there, patches burned black by the napalm. By 1630 they were back in the perimeter. Flody had read all the signs and concluded that the show was all but over.

Alpha Company, after waiting until Charley Company was well beyond shooting distance, moved out as a body, parolling at first toward the southwest. The route took them through what Lieutenant Weindel described as "the thickest clearing I ever busted through in my life." The stand of scrub was less than head-high, but so dense that they had to wield their machetes all the way. Next they entered a sea of elephant grass where the stand rose 10 to 12 feet, an extraordinary growth even for Vietnam. Quite suddenly, the terrain became very rough.

Specialist 4 Stanley A. Wysocki, 20, of Freeland, Pa., was at the extreme end of Third Platoon, on the right flank, with his machine gun. He stood at the edge of a deep ravine. Because the company had halted briefly, he took the M-60 off safety and rested it, so as to cover the ravine. Seconds later, he saw a file of North Vietnamese emerge from the brush and start across his front, within the ravine. So he fired, though they were an indistinct target, more than 250 meters distant. Weindel called in 4.2-mortar fire on them and all five of the 81-mm. mortars also got busy. More than 50 rounds of mortar were

spent that way in the next 10 minutes. At the end, one
Vietnamese came running directly toward Wysocki's
gun, upward through the elephant grass that covered the
slope. Wysocki shot him down, range 15 feet, the only
enemy they could be certain they had killed.

Veering north and moving on a short distance, Alpha
Company, almost without realizing it, entered an NVA
base camp, a veritable spider web of bunkers and huts,
planted amid dense vegetation, thick with thorn trees
and wait-a-minute vines. There were numerous hang-
ups as they tried to bull through. "I don't like this a
damned bit," Weindel said. "We should back away
from it."

The way soon opened. A command ship circled
overhead with a message: "There is a downed chopper
500 meters to your right, with survivors. Get them out."
They went that way only to be thwarted. As they got to
within 50 meters of the Huey, they saw a Chinook lift
upward from the trees directly ahead. Three of the survivors were aboard. The Huey was a total wreck—just
so much junk.

The Chinook radioed, "There is a captain from this
party roaming around somewhere. He went out to look
for water." So the company spent two and a half futile
hours beating the bushes in search of him. It was still
trying hard when there came another message: "Break
off the search. We have him." Lieutenant Colonel
Royce, commanding officer of the 52nd Aviation Battalion, had set forth in another Chinook, found the lost
captain, and hooked him aloft in a basket.

There was still another downed Huey to be succored,
so their task went on and on. They were beating through
dense brush all the way, with much hacking to do. A
chopper flew above them, popping smoke to show them
the way. At 1400 they found what they sought—four

men dead, burned black and blown 20 feet from the aircraft when it exploded; the ship was another total
wreck. A fifth corpse, blackened, was in the wreckage.
It took five stretchers and 20 men to collect the five
bodies and move them out to a clearing 200 meters
away, where they would rendezvous with several choppers that were bringing out body bags. But that short
haul killed another hour. The bush was as impenetrable
as primary jungle; it was hack, hack, hack with
machetes every foot of the way. They got there steam-
ing, sweating, and angry, not because of the work, but
from sight of the five bodies.

At the edge of the clearing, they ran into a tunnel
complex. Other men saw a North Vietnamese duck into
a hole. S.Sgt. Robert F. Wright somehow missed the
motion. He grenaded into another hole, heard a man
scream somewhere below, crawled into the hole, finished the job with his Colt .45, then dragged forth the
body. "I got the son-of-a-bitch," he yelled.

Weindel was feeling leery; just to look at the position
got his wind up. The bodies had been loaded and the
Hueys had cleared away. "I think we better back away
from here in a hell of a hurry," he said to the others.
The men moved out about 300 meters and he called for
the artillery to stonk the place. It was a waste of ammunition; the shells had little or no effect.

The column slogged on. The light was waning fast. So
the company turned back toward the perimeter and
moved as rapidly as the going and its own state of extreme fatigue permitted. As it hove almost within sight
of the base, so did a Huey bearing Lt. Douglas Bennett,
USMA '64, an assistant operations officer from battalion.

"That HMG [heavy machine gun] that knocked down
the Hueys is only about 200 meters from where you

finished your searching this afternoon," Bennett said. "You're to go get it."

Weindel protested. "It's too late," he said. "Dark will be on us and we don't know what's out here."

Bennett insisted. So they went.

After another 600-meter march through thick brush, the men found what they wanted, almost. It was pure dumb luck that they stumbled across the position, marked by a mortar sight, a cradle, six rucksacks, and numerous other trinkets—but no machine gun. Colonel Lay flew out in a Chinook to relieve them of these treasures.

The time was now 1730 and the company was 1,200 meters from its appointed nighttime position. The men started marching through heavily cratered ground where obviously both the artillery and the B-52 bombers had laid it on a bit thick. That slowed them still more and Weindel realized they'd never make it home before dark.

The lieutenant was in front of the column, and, leading off, had not gone more than 50 meters, when loud shouting came from the rear. He couldn't distinguish a word of it. Then he heard a clear voice over his radio telephone: "Lieutenant, get going fast. We're being mortared."

Wright was bringing up the rear of the column, along with First Sergeant Crouse and Lieutenant Quann. All three jumped as the first shell exploded amid the tall timber of a wood patch they had just come through. The burst, 50 meters behind them, was a powerful stimulant.

Immediately, Quann got a message over the RT from an unidentified voice at the base camp: "We're being mortared."

Quann replied, "And so are we."

Lieutenant Dukes, the artillery FO with Quann, called the fire direction center at base camp, saying, "We need fire to cover our rear." He made a snap guess on the coordinates of the column's position. His request, a safety measure, was also an invitation to waste artillery. No skirmishers dogged their heels, and the mortar shells were coming from inside Cambodia, about 1,000 meters to their rear.

Men up front started to double-time. Weindel was all against it and tried to hold them back. He could see mortar shells exploding in sheets to their front, either inside the perimeter or just short of it. The cry was raised: "Move along! Move along!" Weindel yelled, "What the hell for? There's no use rushing into that." Weindel switched to a half-step.

About then, Quann called for a halt, so that he could make a head count. Weindel breathed easier. It seemed like the best possible idea at the time. They were still 700 meters away from the base camp.

So they counted, and found that all hands were present. They started again. Men down the column began to move at a dog trot, and Weindel could not slow them. They puffed along "high diddle, diddle, straight down the middle," as Weindel later put it. Five hundred meters short of the perimeter, they came to their last hill. Topping the crest, they saw four North Vietnamese mortars, directly to their left, set in the low ground, not more than 200 meters away. They were set at the edge of a wood line and were pumping out shells at the rate of four or five a minute, all aimed at the heart of Charley Company. The column kept running. On a knob just beyond a small ridge saddle, Weindel checked long enough to shoot an azimuth at the NVA position. It was 060 from where he stood.

For a minute or so a dip in the contour of the land

almost swallowed them. Racing on, they topped a small rise. Then a burst of M-16 rifle fire from out of the perimeter crackled just above their heads. Weindel shouted, "Everybody halt!" and hit the dirt.

At first Captain Flody and the others had stopped all fire at the base, just to make sure that the incoming stuff was from the enemy. In these same moments, Quann called Lieutenant Eastwood on the RT. "Take it easy," he said. "We're coming in." The warning had to go the complete circle because Charley Company had spread itself to man Alpha Company's foxholes, also.

The first enemy round fired in their direction had exploded at 1810. Flody saw the round—that one round only—explode 200 meters to his southeast. Then they came on in twos and threes and he heard them whistle on the downpath into the ground immediately around him.

Colonel Lay was still airborne in the Chinook and orbiting around the LZ. So were two of his staff, Bigelow and Bennett, who followed along in a Huey. Someone on the ground told them over the RT, "Don't land! There's too much fire." The stuff was coming in bunches now. Bigelow and Bennett took the warning seriously, veered off in their Huey, and headed for Pleijerang, where they listened to the battle over the radio. Not so Colonel Lay.

Running for the operations center, Flody found Lay there. The Chinook had dropped him. Lay had spent several minutes in a foxhole observing, and he was full of fresh information.

"Range is about 2,000 meters," he said to Flody. "I'd say the bearing is around 290."

Just then the battalion S-2, Lt. C. Downs, spoke up. "I'm talking to an FAC right now. He sees them firing. I have the coordinates."

They checked. The figures were roughly congruent with the estimate Lay had just made by dead reckoning. They pointed to Hill 421, right on the Cambodian border and directly to the northwest.

But the coordinates did not relate at all to the mortars that Weindel had just seen blasting the perimeter. That was what they missed at first—that they were being barraged from two mortar bases, one far out and one close by. It was not within the scope of combined intelligence to grasp the essential fact. Hard beset by the blows they were getting, they could not distinguish between one sound and another. Here was the small thing that nearly did them in.

In this worst of moments Flody discovered that he had no communications with his gun positions. One mortar round had cut the wire. So he started for the guns on a run, knowing that they all had to be turned about. He passed the first tube and yelled to the crew. "Swing it around 300 mils!" Continuing to gun No. 2, he was hit and knocked down by a mortar shard that slashed open one cheek of his buttocks. Paying no attention to the bleeding, he made the rounds, getting the guns turned.

As the fifth gun completed the turning movement, Flody heard a yell, "Cease fire! A Company is getting hit." It was completely wrong. Not understanding what the yell meant, Flody passed the warning along, shouting: "Cease fire with all weapons!" The command raced around the circle as madly as a latrine rumor.

Specialist 4 Sensenbach, with three of his buddies, had just sat down to play a friendly game of stud poker by candlelight. That's when the first mortar round exploded into their ground shortly after the battalion commander's arrival in the Chinook at the northwest corner. Sensenbach heard Colonel Lay's voice ring out loud and clear above the tumult, "Oh shit!" "There goes our poker game," said Sensenbach, a 26-year-old from Tetonia, Idaho, a country boy and proud of it, strongly built, with sandy hair and very twinkly eyes.

Some of the men were still in the open, including Lieutenant Dresia. There was a reason: the mail had just come in, heavy with premature Christmas gifts. This group heard the first round explode about 100 meters away. Still, they stuck with it. The three soldiers distributing packages were coming straight toward them. Spec. 4 Jerry Knox, an artillery FO, let out a joyous yeep, "Gee, everybody's making it this time." A mortar shell exploded within a hop-skip-and-jump of where they stood. "Get to the holes, everybody!" Dresia yelled.

It was a little late. Shells rained on them. Dresia's RTO, Pfc. Joseph Blackwell, was killed outright. The aid man of the platoon, Spec. 4 Allen Courtney, took wounds in the chest and shoulders. A second round exploded dead on one of Dresia's machine-gun positions, destroying the gun and instantly killing the gunners, Specialist 4 Fulmer and Private First Class Bocook. In the hole with them was their squad leader, S.Sgt. William J. Grandy Jr. of Philadelphia. Hit in the head, Grandy had blacked out from concussion.

Hard hit but not downed, Courtney heard a cry from farther along the foxhole line: "Medic! Medic!" He went that way. In the hole with Spec. 4 Richard T. Carey, a 22-year-old from Watkinsville, Ga., was Pfc. Theodore Washington, a 20-year-old Virginian. A very solemn soldier, Carey never wastes a word or a motion. His face was a mask of blood. Washington had been hit in the left elbow, legs, and stomach. Courtney knelt and patched them as best he could. Neither said a word. As Courtney rose to continue his rounds, Spec. 4 Roosevelt

President, a 21-year-old South Carolinian, staggered into the position. President was drenched in blood, hit in both shoulders, head, and back. Courtney went to work on him.

Corporal Cecil Walker had tarried just a second too long hoping to get goodies from home. As he jumped for the hole next to Dresia's a shell exploded right behind him, caught him in midair, and killed him. He had been closer to the foxhole than anyone else.

Specialist 4 Dennis P. Sullivan, an 18-year-old from New York City, was worried because Fulmer's machine gun wasn't going. Quitting his foxhole, he crawled that way to see what was wrong. Another round exploded while he was still crawling and one shard smashed his right hand.

At a second machine-gun position, the assistant, Pfc. Leon Anderson of Seattle, was killed instantly. Pvt. Felton Anderson, a 21-year-old from Houston, was wounded in the head. One big hunk of metal had smashed the right hand of Specialist 4 Capps.

The cry "Medic! Medic!" became almost incessant. Still, there was no panic and some of the wounded did not cry at all, a few too sorely stricken to do so, the more lightly wounded knowing they would have to wait. With two of the aid men already down, Spec. 4 George Richardson and Spec. 4 Will Stewart were all over the place, bandaging here, giving a shot of morphine there.

Two rounds fell among the 81-mm. mortars. Spec. 4 Roger J. Schlott, hit in the back, was the only casualty for the moment. The 81's were still firing.

Captain Flody made a quick estimate, or mental note, "We're already cut to half-strength," and in that reckoning he might well have included himself. He had arrived at the artillery fire direction center badly winded, and, as he paused for breath, another mortar shell exploded behind him, riddled his back, and knocked him flat. He thought he was blacking out from concussion. His mind cleared as the shelling ceased, and he stood.

So doing, he thought things over. Within eight minutes approximately 25 rounds of 82-mm. mortar had been fired by the enemy and not one had missed the perimeter. By these signs, Flody knew what he was up against. The absolute accuracy could not be attributed to skilled observation only. The enemy battery had previously registered on this ground and knew that the mortars were set dead-on. There were no adjustments to be made. It was like shooting fish in a barrel.

In the brief lull, the worst cases were carried to the aid station so that they could be given plasma. Also, the position was reorganized, so that there would be better distribution foxhole to foxhole. Carey was one of the cases put on plasma. When the shelling resumed, one of the first rounds blasted him from his pallet. He still lived, though the spark was feeble, and there were fresh wounds in his back and left eye.

The second time around, the main target was the artillery. Spec. 4 James T. Fore, 20, from San Leandro, Calif., was assistant gunner on the base piece. One shard hit him in the neck. He ducked away for five minutes, returned with his neck bandaged, and said, "I'm just as good as ever." Several minutes later, Spec. 4 Carl Treahan, 21, of Willimantic, Conn., was hit in the back while on No. 5 gun. After getting bandaged, he found he could no longer stand without bleeding badly, so he worked the rest of the night in the FDC.

Flody, by this time reeling from loss of blood and the concussion, knew that he was through. "You're in command of the battery," he said to Lt. Frank M. Applin, 24, of Providence, R.I.

Applin asked, "You got something to tell me?"

"It's all yours," Flody said. "You take it away."

"Right!" Applin replied.

Considering the circumstances, the low key, the undramatic pitch of this dialogue may be worth repeating, if only that it might give some novelist pause in the future, though this is doubtful. Five minutes later Flody had blacked out.

In these moments, Lieutenant Swan, commanding Third Platoon, was running back to his foxhole. Swan is a 25-year-old son of Hammond, Ind., schooled at the University of Wisconsin. Three words—short, trim, peppery—fit him perfectly.

A mortar round beat Swan to the hole. One shard had slashed the left eye of Pfc. Kenneth W. Jones, a Philadelphian, and the platoon medic, Spec. 4 Robert Page, a 21-year-old Pittsburgher, had his kit open, preparing to work on Jones. Luck had been with Pfc. Robert A. Miles, 21, from Skokie, Ill., an FO with the 81-mm. mortars. The blast had blown him from the hole, but he scrambled back unhurt. Page gave Jones a shot of morphine. Swan sank down in the hole, then sat up straight, figuring he had better look about. A mortar round exploded seven meters behind the hole. Swan had twisted to look that way. One shard struck him in the right teat, the other in the left shoulder. His sensation was one of "being flattened by a baseball bat." The blast flattened him across Jones and Miles, and the squeeze knocked the wind from them. Swan knew concussion: he was too dizzy to think. The three just lay there. Hearing a cry, "Medic, Medic," Page had departed.

A second round, arriving at the same time, took out four other members of the platoon. Spec. 4 David N. Gaither, 22, of Baltimore was hit in the back of the head; Spec. 4 Robert E. Hollon, 21, an Alabaman, got a shard through his back; Pfc. Edward Matlack, 20, of Cleveland was hit in the throat; another 20-year-old Ohioan, Spec. 4 Hubert Linscott, was hit in the shoulder.

A funny thing about Linscott: he had previously been hit by a bullet without knowing it. The slug had lodged in his right hip. He had no sensation at the time. There was no way of accounting for how and where it happened. The wound was not discovered until the next day. While hardly commonplace, this often happens in battle.

At the artillery site, Lt. Jack L. Stewart, the fire direction officer, heard the thuds and crashes as the mortar shells beat on the camp, and felt better about it than anyone else. Not only were his guns working, but instinct and training also told him that his shells were finding pay dirt. The enemy fire was gradually tapering off. However, Stewart, concentrating on his job, also noted from the sounds, still not seeing any flash, that at least one enemy mortar was operating from much closer range. (This was the battery that Weindel had seen from atop the hill.) He said to himself, ''We'll let the 81's go to work on that one.'' There was no further time for thought. Just then his guns came under machine-gun fire and he judged that the gun was based even closer than the mortar. It was much too close.

Alpha Company, meanwhile, was in the act of closing on the perimeter, and there was no need for it to be prodded. It was not, however, the sight of the perimeter being mortared that drew the men on; they couldn't do a bit of good for Charley Company simply by sharing part of its misery. The sprint was on so that they could get to their own foxholes. Weindel, who by this time had become a war-horse with bells on his collar, was in an agony of mind even when running. Ahead, he could see what the close-in enemy mortar battery was dealing out to the sector held by Swan's platoon. For two seconds, while he had paused on top of the hill, he had weighed whether he should attack those same mortars, so close and just off his flank. Then he had dismissed the thought, saying to himself, "We need to get there fast; a direct assault may be coming." Now the question nagged him, "Was I right? Was I right?" He would never really know.

Wearing horseshoes all the way, Alpha Company made it, out of wind and virtually unhurt. The time was 1845. The only casualty was S.Sgt. John E. Brown, who took a light flesh wound in one thigh from a mortar frag while he was jumping a ditch. Irritated when he found Charley Company's men filling some of the holes toward which his men were dashing under fire, Weindel yelled, "Get the hell out of here and go where you belong." They got. As Weindel settled in his own hole, he saw a new enemy mortar open fire from the southeast.

Specialist 4 Rodger M. Sanker, 20, of Philsburg, Pa., an assistant machine gunner with Third Platoon, found his hole at the same time. He saw two mortars firing from the northeast; the shells were going over Able Company's sector and breaking amid Charley Company. "They're about 800 meters away," he said to the other men, referring to the mortars. "They're inside a wood line which I saw coming down. So don't waste your ammo." By Sanker's measure, the rounds came on steadily, about four to the minute.

Still, the manner in which this reinforcement was made proved how true the saying is that half the easements of life double its aggravations. The hair-shirt fell on one of Charley Company's two-man outposts. In the excitement, the outposts had not been recalled; in-

deed, they were all but forgotten. Worse still, at least
one of them had not been advised that Alpha Company
was arriving. This OP was 40 meters out on the right
flank of Charley Company.

Private First Class Santos Villareal saw dark forms
charging toward him through the dusk. Villareal, 20, is
from Port Isabel, Tex., a real charmer—short, dark,
with a handsome face lighted by a perpetual grin. With
him was an 18-year-old Maine lad, Pfc. Stewart L.
Shedd. They were armed only with M-79 grenade
launchers.

With every reason to be stampeded, they held their
ground and their nerve, keeping low behind a rosewood
log.

The front runners were just 30 meters away, coming
straight for the OP, when Shedd asked, "Shall we let
'em have it?"

"No, we can't," Villareal said very low. "We don't
know who they are."

Some instinct told him, or perhaps it was the size of
the blurred forms, that these must be Americans. Still,
they kept their M-79's pointed.

It had taken Alpha Company perhaps two minutes to
run past them. The column closed, Sgt. Paul Johansen
yelling as he went by, "I'm the last man from A Company."

Wiping the sweat from his face on the sleeve of his
jungle shirt, Villareal said to Shedd, "Thank God,
that's over."

But what had happened still worried him; he had
realized in those tense moments that grenade launchers
were not the weapons to stop a skirmish line. So he tried
to raise Lieutenant Swan on the RT to tell him that a few
M-16 rifles were needed at the position.

However, it was 1st Sgt. Francisco C. Paredo, 31, of Guam who responded on the radio. Quite terse about it, Paredo replied flatly, "No, you don't need rifles out there."

Five minutes passed. The two listeners heard more noise, more men coming in over exactly the same line Alpha Company had followed. Now it was too dark to see anything. The noises came closer—15 feet, 12 feet. At 10 feet, Villareal saw in silhouette a form wearing a peaked cap and knew it was a Vietnamese. A yell came from the figure: "I'm A Company. I'm A Company."

Making the fastest draw ever out of Port Isabel, Villareal plugged the man in the belly with his Colt .45, then shot twice more as the man lay crumbled on the ground.

Now in standing position, Villareal could see 10 to 12 more Vietnamese beyond the body, coming on. He turned to run. Shedd had already taken off, leaving the PRC-25 behind. Villareal also forgot all about the radio.

Ten meters along the trail, the thought hit him: "They'll shoot me in the back." He whirled, dropped to his knees, and fired one M-79 round. It armed and exploded among the enemy group, which had already hit the ground. Villareal ran on. As he made the perimeter, he jumped into the nearest foxhole. In it was Pfc. Daniel S. Marshall, 21, of Bridgeport, Conn. Villareal's ammunition for the launcher, other than what had been abandoned at the OP, was in his own foxhole, some distance away. He opted to go for it because "our people seemed too jumpy."

"VC coming on, from that direction," he said to Marshall. "You better fire."

Marshall just barely started. Then his M-16 jammed.

The position now weaponless, Villareal ran toward the artillery battery where he borrowed an M-14 from one of the wounded.

Apart from the damage wrought by the renewal of the mortar attack, which lasted about 10 minutes, the condition within the perimeter was becoming increasingly chaotic and dangerous. The battery had been firing for most of an hour. It was impossible to both work the howitzers, which were rather sketchily dug in, and at the same time insure easy movement through the piled-up litter. There was no time to police it. Powder bags and shells were strewn all over the place. Then, too, the Chinooks had come in and dropped 450 rounds of ammunition, most of it HE, on the edge of the landing zone just before the fight began. Not more than 100 high explosive rounds had been brought into the circle and fed the guns. Three piles of shells, indifferently stacked, lay just outside the foxhole line. Having a sort of premonitory glimpse of what might happen, Lieutenant Stewart brooded about this, but could do nothing.

Lieutenant Swan, who had shaken himself into semi-recovery, and was again observing from his foxhole, saw a North Vietnamese wiggle forward into the ground where the Chinooks had dumped the ammunition.

Specialist Sensenbach saw him, also. The enemy soldier was not more than 25 meters away; then Sensenbach saw him flatten behind a log. The Idaho boy let go at the target with an M-60, but the burst merely riddled the wood.

Villareal saw the Vietnamese, just the flash of an arm. He fired with his M-14. Result: negative.

Swan had already opened fire with his M-16. Other riflemen joined him; it was a strong distraction. Then Swan saw an arm rise up from the log and throw something in the direction of the canisters. It sputtered and flamed as it arched, and it looked like either a grenade or a trip flare. The first shell pile blazed.

The explosion had fired the fiberboard containers. Next, the brass containers for the powder charges went off, and within a few seconds the whole thing was blowing, strewing hot metal from end to end of the perimeter. The 105-mm. rounds did not explode, but the blast from the brass containers picked them up and hurled them as so many projectiles against the tented camp. The exploding mass was about six meters by fifteen in area. The flames made the camp bright as day. Weindel, who was at least 40 meters from the center of the holocaust, saw one shell arc 50 feet above his head.

Lieutenant Frank D. Willis, 25, of Meadowbrook, Pa., led the battalion's 4.2-mortar platoon. His tubes had put out 30 rounds against the enemy mortar positions in their first 10 minutes of action. Then the ammo pile blew. Willis' tent was 150 meters from the blast. He thought he was fairly safe. But flying metal shredded his tent. One shard cut a hole the size of a basketball. Another wounded Spec. 4 Roger Schwartz, a 21-year-old Chicagoan.

The fight itself, as such, passed from their minds, and they all but forgot the enemy. All around the perimeter men were digging frantically, deepening the foxholes. There was more than a small bit of panic in this; the thing had happened to them so suddenly, so unexpectedly, that even the men nearest the scene who had observed how it all started could not think calmly about it or explain it to others. Sensenbach stayed doubled in his foxhole, head between his knees, in crash position. "If I am going to live," he thought, "then I don't dare raise my head." The heat was terrible; he was just 25 meters from the exploding mass.

Captain Flody was again conscious, dully aware that something unusual was going on, though at first he could not figure it out. He sat amid the battery, staring at the No. 1 gun. It was a wreck. The last enemy mortar round had exploded under it and destroyed the piece. Members of the gun crew had nipped back just in time to save themselves.

Less than a minute had passed. Now, as Flody watched, one great hunk of metal from the exploding mass hit into the piled-up 105-mm. shells next to the ruined gun. There must have been 70 rounds of the stuff, and the whole thing blew.

Of the eight men working the gun, six were hit trying to get away from the spot. Spec. 4 James McFarland, a cook who had come up to pass ammunition, took a sliver of steel in his left arm. Pfc. Joseph Liciandrello of Binghamton, N.Y., was hit in the left hand, and Pfc. Robert Carulli, also of Binghamton, took a shard in his back. A piece of 105 shell went through the left biceps of Pfc. Harry Carter of Oklahoma City. Pfc. John Overmire, a Utah boy, was hit in the tail. Cpl. Robert Skomra got his in the left thigh. All were dazed by the calamity and shocked by the coincidence—that within a few seconds the gun and its men were together dealt out by two blows little related to one another.

For all of one hour this was the condition of the perimeter; all hands staying as low as possible, making no use of weapons, striving only to escape the burning metal that was scything the grass all about. There were more losses before the small inferno stuttered to a halt. In Swan's platoon, Winscott and Villareal were wounded for a second time. Sgt. Florencia M. Abad of Bremerton, Wash., had his right hand smashed by a large piece of brass. Pfc. Cornelius Roberson, 21, of Seattle was hit in the right arm. Spec. 4 Richard O.

McKinnie, 21, of Cleveland was hit in the left shoulder.

They had never imagined that things could be like this in the field. They had heard about control all through training, but were told nothing of the possibility that fate may sometimes intervene to make reaction uncontrollable. With them, as with all others, it is a lesson learned the hard way. Each man had the queer feeling of being lost with people all around him. Villareal was one such. He kept muttering to himself, "What the hell, what the hell." He was as afraid as when, on running from the outpost, he had expected death in the next second; but, unlike then, he was now thoroughly confused by what had occurred.

Through all this time, the one outpost where Specialist 4 McKinnie was in charge had stayed together, forgotten by everyone else, and quite content initially to remain 40 meters distant from the main shooting gallery. McKinnie is a very small Negro, a natural joker whose sense of humor bubbles when other men need it most.

When the mortaring started, Pfc. Colin J. MacKeigin, a 20-year-old fellow Clevelander, asked McKinnie, "Don't you think we better go on in?"

"Don't you know when you're well off?" McKinnie replied. "I like it out here."

That was good for the minute. Shortly afterward the mortars shifted their line slightly. Frags cut the elephant grass not far from where they lay. "It looks," McKinnie said, "as if they're walking those shells straight for me."

MacKeigin spoke again, "Do you feel the same way as you did?"

"No, man," McKinnie said. "It's running time now."

He took off at a sprint and MacKeigin hightailed it

behind him. They dove for the first bunker they saw; it was empty, 20 meters out in front of the perimeter, though they didn't know that then.

McKinnie, looking about, saw Lieutenant Dresia signaling with his arm from the closest foxhole.

"Do you need help?" McKinnie called.

"All I can get," said Dresia.

Both men started. Dresia yelled, "One of you stay there." MacKeigin turned back.

McKinnie slid toward the foxhole just beyond Dresia. In it were two dead men "all messed up." McKinnie stared, shocked by what he saw, but still so fascinated that he couldn't take his eyes away. Then he retched violently, and for five minutes he lay there heaving. Once his mind and stomach cleared, he ran back to rejoin MacKeigin.

An M-60 began firing from about 30 meters to their rear. First the bullets whipped very close over their heads, then cut into the sandbags just above them.

"Looks to me as if we're still way out in front," said MacKeigin.

"Man," said McKinnie, "I think you're crazy."

The machine gun sputtered, then quit. McKinnie looked about him. "Man, you sure as hell are right. Let us get mobile."

They ran for the nearest foxhole to the other side of Dresia. It was already filled to capacity, three men in it. Even so, they jumped for it. Washington, already wounded, was one of the occupants.

Another soldier, Specialist 4 Hightower, said, "Too many men in this hole. Somebody gotta get out."

"Man, it won't be us," McKinnie said. "We just got here."

"Never mind," said Pfc. Willie J. Williams, 21, of New York City. "I'll start digging again."

A real accommodating soldier, Williams went to work, plying two entrenching spades at one time.

Although they urged him to leave, Washington insisted on staying in the hole. McKinnie had felt him over, found the body stiffening, and thought this might be a sign that the end was approaching. It didn't occur to him that, cramped as they all were, and wounded as Washington was, he wouldn't likely stay supple. Fifteen minutes passed. By then, Williams, almost finished with the widening of the hole, and feeling good about it, was singing very loudly "The Battle of New Orleans." It perked them all up, including Washington.

Hightower, who had been observing to the front, said, "I see a gook machine gun firing out there." He pointed it out to the others; the gun was about 300 meters away. "Do you think you can hit it?" he asked McKinnie.

"I don't know," McKinnie said. "I never fired a machine gun in my life."

But he started, and was a splendid success. It took him 250 rounds, but he knocked out the gun.

That made them all feel better. Washington spoke up. He was willing to try for the aid station, provided Willie J., the workhorse, would half-carry him there. Williams was willing.

"Man," McKinnie said to Washington, "I guess you reached the point where you were feeling stiff enough."

So the three who remained settled back. It was about that moment, as Washington made the aid station, that McKinnie stood in the foxhole to see how things were doing elsewhere. That's when the first ammo pile exploded. A large hunk of brass hit McKinnie between the shoulder blades, split open his back, and sprawled him across the others.

Throughout the hour when the showering metal laid

them low (and, by the way, none of it bothered Alpha
Company), the position might have disintegrated completely had the enemy mortar attack resumed. But the
mortars were through. Either all the shells had been
fired, or the air strikes, which promptly followed the 4.2
bombardment laid on by Lieutenant Willis, had completed their elimination. The air came in low with
rockets and napalm, and Willis saw the stuff blast and
burn the target area, dead center. The planes out of
Pleiku and Tuy Hoa made 108 sorties that night. Some
of the runs were close, too close, to the defending line;
Sergeant Breaux, the operations staff, got hit in the
back with a cluster bomb unit. For the most part,
however, the air strikes were laid on to seal off the
escape routes—trails and stream beds—between the
combat field and the Cambodian border, 1,000 meters
to the west. Most of the artillery, operating from the
more distant bases, and firing 5,000 rounds before the
cease-fire was given, had the same object. Even that distant part of the show, however, cost high. Two gunships
went down in flames within sight of the men in the foxholes.

As the blast gradually cooled, Sensenbach responded.
He could raise his head and look around a bit, which
made him feel better. So doing, he saw a figure rise
from behind the rosewood log and stand long enough in
the clear light. Sensenbach put his M-16 to his shoulder
and sighted carefully. His hand was steady as he pulled
the trigger. Five bullets and the figure toppled over.
Sensenbach said to himself, "I got him, I got the guy
that did it," and felt great satisfaction.

But there was really no way of knowing whether it
was the same man. Suddenly there were other blurred
figures moving from the darkness into the circle of light.

Some moved to within 10 meters or so of the log and began digging. At the same time Weindel's Third Platoon in Alpha Company came under attack. The time was about 1930. The North Vietnamese could be seen clear enough in silhouette, due to the slowly dying fire outside the perimeter. They were all elaborately camouflaged; at close range, they appeared as well-fed, healthy soldiers. But they were also exhausted men, going through the motions, and no longer possessed of the heart to fight. They dug languidly and they fired aimlessly, though they were close enough to use grenades. Their half of the fight was more like sham battle than the real thing. Our half wasn't; the enemy had moved close enough to get killed. So for another hour, another unequal contest, this time balanced entirely against the enemy, went on. The fire fight in slow motion continued until 2130, then flickered out in just about the same minute as the blazing pile beyond the perimeter turned to ashes. Men let their tired minds and bodies relax.

Not one American was killed or wounded in the final round. Thirty-four enemy bodies were counted just outside the foxhole line when morning light came. The battalion reported officially a body count of 76; it was a pardonable exaggeration and much closer to the truth. They were not exultant. Although, to one another, they made no victory claim for themselves after having their ears pinned back for so long, they nonetheless knew, without higher-ups having to tell them, that it was anything other than a defeat. They had held their ground through it all. The enemy had tried not only to smash them, but also to squeeze them out. He had partly succeeded in the one thing and completely failed in the other. The men knew which side had not only withdrawn from the battlefield but also retreated to sanctuary where it could not be hurt.

Two battalions of the 88th NVA Regiment had been thrown into the attack, their mission being to "destroy an American landing zone." Their report to higher headquarters admitted failure.

But the two companies did not know this when they patrolled up to the Cambodian border on the following morning. They were elated on hearing a POW report some days later. Reading, they felt better about the whole thing.

The author, with Maj. Gen. Keith L. Ware of the First Infantry Division, *left*, who died in action Sept. 13, 1968.

The author interviews survivors after a battle.

Sgt. 1st Cl. Normal A. Doney of Special Forces, *on left at top*, with the team he led into enemy territory.

Riflemen deploy from a Huey in the Highlands.

Trooper examines RPG-7 rocket similar to the one that brought down the Husky inside Charley Company's position. The rocket is made in the Soviet Union.

Machine gunners in action on an M-60 in the Central Highlands. The standardized 7.62-mm weapon was employed extensively by American troops in Vietnam, though the number of rounds carried with it varied.

Lt. Col. Eleazar Parmly IV, the outspoken commander of the Civilian Irregular Defense Group camps in the far west Highlands, doubted rumor of enemy attack.

Some of Parmly's civilian irregulars line up for inspection at the Pleijerang camp.

One of his squads plunges through the tall elephant grass.

Task Force Prong preparing to leave LZ Lane. In the tiger suit is Capt. David D. Casto. Next to him is Col. Judson Miller, commanding officer of the Second Brigade, Fourth Division. Kneeling in the corner at right is Spec. 4 John E. Mitchell, who had just 32 days to go before returning home. He was killed an hour later.

The mountainous border area beyond the Plei Trap Valley, as seen in an aerial photograph taken from an American plane. Terrain is rough, difficult to maneuver over. U.S. forces relied on helicopters to move troops.

Army Chinook arrives with cargo at hilltop post.

Scout dog hunts Vietcong.

GI, his soft fatigue hat camouflaged with leaves, holds aloft red smoke canister to guide in air support. Heavy jungle makes air surveillance difficult along border.

Typical mountaintop battalion fire base carved out of country-side by U.S. troops. This one, of 4th Division, is close to Cambodia. Sandbags protect gun sites and bunkers from incoming mortar fire.

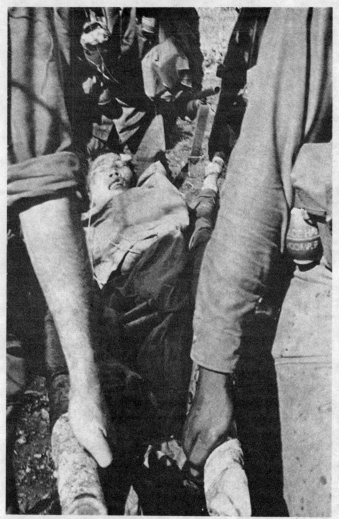

Wounded North Vietnamese prisoner is carried back by U.S. troops on stretcher for medical treatment and questions by intelligence officers.

The Illusory Fight————

The two rifle companies had been in the field since 26 September without starting anything monumental or worth writing home about. The one big battalion fight had been a rescue mission ending in a real zapping.

Considering that this was now 2 December, 1966, and all the while they had been in the western Central Highlands, near enough to thumb noses at the Cambodian border, they had proper reason to feel either out of luck, or itchy, restive, and misused.

That the morning was glorious, clear-skied, and freshed by a slight breeze gave them no cheer. They were as indifferent to weather as to the fact that they had camped in a pleasantly green and not too rough or jungle-clad sector of the unfamiliar plateau. The few ridges were neither steep nor heavily rock-strewn. The area was clad with low bush and elephant grass. But there was little difficulty getting about. The trails, which wended in all directions, were numerous, and one out of six or so looked well beaten.

The maneuver set for that morning did not appear difficult as Lt. Brendan T. Quann and his platoon commanders once again went over the map just before breaking camp. Quann commanded Alpha Company, First Battalion, 12th Infantry. The night had been spent in perimeter on Hill 346 (coordinates 548-543), which overlooked the battalion's artillery support base. Fifteen hundred meters to the north, on another hill, Bravo Company of the same battalion had bivouacked without incident.

Now they were to start marching at the same time, moving roughly southwestward on gradually converging axes that should bring them together somewhere around 1100 on another piece of high ground 1,700 meters away.

The ridge marked as their objective was the only conspicuous terrain feature, at least so the map said. The countryside between was dotted by a few small hills, but as far as the eye could see the land was sparsely vegetated. South Vietnam is not all jungle. Their mission was the usual thing—search and destroy.

"It should be a straight march," said Quann. "Without problems." And that is how it looked to his junior lieutenants.

Alpha Company got under way at exactly 0730, Quann and 106 other soldiers. They went heavily laden but not overloaded by the standards of field forces in Vietnam. The riflemen toted an average of 500 rounds for each M-16, two frag grenades and one smoke, two canteens, and two meals. Distributed between the machine gunners and ammo bearers for each M-60 were 1,100 rounds. The M-79 grenadiers were packing 42 rounds for each launcher. Besides these burdens, five claymore mines were spread around each squad. The company had left its mortars at base camp.

When they started, the artillery fired a few smoke rounds to their front and off the flanks of the line they were to take, simply to set a pattern for the march.

With Bravo Company, which was more distant from the fire base, the artillery had a better thing going. At first the difference was of little interest to the column of Alpha Company, which had its own row to hoe and had become sweated through by the first hour and mile. This changed abruptly within the next 15 minutes, by which time the column had advanced approximately 1,250 meters.

Alpha Company was already within clear sight of the objective ridge and Bravo Company was somewhere to its rear. No hint from intelligence had indicated that real trouble lay ahead.

At that point Quann halted his company. He was worried that the high explosive shells intended to provide a covering curtain for Bravo's troops as they slogged along would endanger his own men as they moved obliquely to the right. He growled over the PRC-25, "Tell those mothers to hold up on the HE."

While they waited, Pfc. Gregg Osborne, an M-79 gunner, got careless. His weapon slipped from his shoulder and, when he grabbed for it, fired. The grenade round bore into the mud next to his foot but did not explode. So they tarried longer while the NCO's moved about explaining to the troops what had happened. They then moved along about 200 meters to the bank of a creek. There another soldier accidentally fired his M-16.

"For an outfit cautioned to be quiet, we're going like a circus," said a machine gunner, Pfc. Horace F. Weight, a tall, gangly 20-year-old redhead from Las Vegas, a farm boy who didn't make it through grade school. He noticed that the others were getting edgy. The company was formed in three columns, which, with the flankers and the points and scouts ahead, gave it the spread of a small city block. Quann called it a "wedge

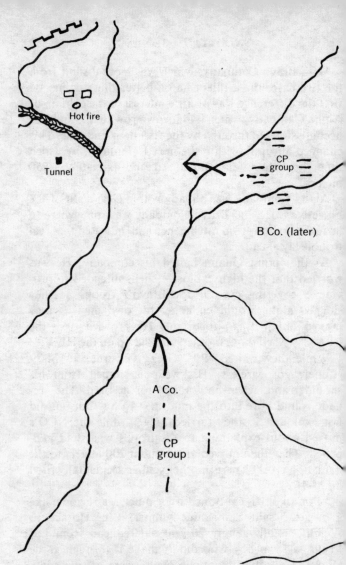

Maze of creeks that Alpha Company and, following it, Bravo Company met. Command Post (CP) groups are in center of each. Tunnel was focus of search.

formation," which was a euphemism. Placed with the center column, Quann could see little of his flanks because of the brush.

The stream confronting Quann was in semiflood, rich with sienna-hued silt that boiled white around the boulders. "Move through slowly," the lieutenant ordered over the radio. "Fill canteens as you go, but keep moving." Few bothered to pick up water. The men, including those on point, waded through in pairs, arms locked, lest the current prove too strong or the water too deep.

When they made the far bank, Quann heard on the radio from Spec. 4 Roger E. Odell, 21, of Lisbon, N.H., the RTO of Third Platoon, on the right flank: "We've come to the creek, clear, smooth water. Looks good for drinking."

This was the first, faint warning to Quann that Alpha Company was heading into a V-shaped confluence of streams, a natural maze of twisting watercourses. It was puzzling, but at this point he could not take it seriously; in the end, the maze was what twisted his wedge beyond control. All three platoons reported they were coming abreast of a creek. Unable to see, Quann could not envisage three different creeks within that fairly limited space. His maps showed no streams whatsoever.

First Platoon, on the left, radioed at that moment that it had come to a creek. Coincidentally, Spec. 4 Robert Ward, on point for Third Platoon on the right, called back, "I see a tunnel ahead of me." Twenty-three-year-old Arthur J. Gipson of Dayton, Ohio, a second lieutenant leading Second Platoon, heard Quann give the order to First Platoon: "Move on up and check out the tunnel." Still, it did not occur to Gipson that things were going wrong and that First Platoon was being ordered to march across Third Platoon's front.

A 22-year-old M-79 gunner, Spec. 4 Shelby R. Stewart of Pineville, Ky., and his buddy, Sammie G. Peak, had heard enough talk about a tunnel. They were in the fore of Third Platoon. Stewart said to Peak, "Let's go see." What they found disgusted them. It was just a "damn loose digging in a bank, big enough for a possum."

Lieutenant Mark N. Enari of Third Platoon, with Odell and Specialist 4 Wysocki, a fire team leader, got up to them a few minutes later and confirmed to Quann that the tunnel was more hallucination than hole. However, Enari, prowling the bushes near the hole, found a rude hut, untenanted, where coals blazed hot, amid other signs of hasty departure. The information came through too late to keep Quann from compounding his error. Having started with the mistaken idea that First Platoon was nearest the tunnel, he had already pressed the unit again to get up to it. The platoon banged ahead, looking for a tunnel without finding it, thus widening its separation from the other elements.

Wysocki, Odell, and others of the fire team marched on and came to another creek. Enari told Peak, "Take the rest of the squad across and join them." Third Squad got on line and prepared to march forward. Enari said to Odell, "Call Sergeant Morris and tell him to move Second Squad across." By the time Plat. Sgt. Roy T. Morris had Second Squad in Motion, Third Squad was 75 meters beyond the creek.

Private First Class Jesse L. Carter, 21, of Oakland, Calif., was the RTO of Third Platoon, and was moving with Second Squad. He had taken three steps into the stream, which was only about 15 meters wide, when he heard automatic weapons firing to his front. He called on his radio company, "I believe this platoon is engaged."

Stewart, Odell, and the other frontrunner had moved to within 20 meters of a line of bunkers without ever seeing anything that signaled danger. The first warning came when they heard a bolt click; instantly, together, they hit the ground.

Specialist 4 Dennis Mumma, the machine gunner, had moved to the fore and was out in the open. The first man to get hit, Mumma took two bullets through both cheeks of his buttocks and one in the abdomen. Luck had to be with him. He continued firing as he called to the others, "Look out for that machine gun!"

Stewart was doing his best to make himself small behind a six-inch sapling. The morale builder-upper of the platoon, he noticed that no one was talking much now and knew that he did not himself feel like doing so. He could clearly see the bunkers as he peered ahead, his eyes six inches above ground level. There were three of them. From his right, a single sniper seemed to be operating from a tree. But the aim was very poor.

Mumma's effort flourished, faltered, and began to fail. The assistant machine gunner, Spec. 4 Larry L. Redcey, hit in the belly, was already out of it. Peak started for the machine gun with the idea of helping Mumma; enroute, he was hit twice in the tail and stopped. It seemed to help Mumma; he resumed firing.

Then loss of blood slowed him. Sgt. George Edmonds noticed it, started toward the machine gun, and took a bullet in his right leg. Downed, he picked himself up again, got to Mumma, placed him about half in defilade —a dip in the ground behind a palm tree—and took over the gun.

Edmonds must have fired all of 50 rounds. The sniper on the right had persisted. Distracted, Edmonds tried to go after him with a grenade. The sniper, until then innocuous, got him first. The bullet drilled him through both shoulders. Edmonds flattened. The medic, Spec. 4 Louis de la Rosa, came up to care for Edmonds and bandaged him under fire. Strange but true, the Army does not pin medals for acts like those of Mumma, Edmonds, and de la Rosa.

Throughout this time, all the rest of the company was nonengaged, the body of the platoon did not understand what was going on, and Quann was unaware that he had a fight on his hands. There is nothing odd or unseemly about this. The others heard the crackling of weapons, diffused by the bush. But they could not guess from the sounds what was happening, or know that a small salient of men, formed by chance through the movement of one squad of the company, was in mortal danger. Each man was doing his duty more or less, though none but the men under direct fire could guess what duty might require of the main body. And this is a commonplace in war.

We know how long they engaged the bunkers virtually in solitude, unhelped by any of the other hands. It was 10 minutes. Throughout that time even the men directly under the machine-gun fire did not realize that the three bunkers were but one segment of a system. The rest of the fortified line—the outer facing of a North Vietnamese Army base camp—did not open fire. Quann and the platoons out of sight of the action remained unaware that anything important had been started. Pfc. Charley M. Alexander, a 22-year-old rifleman from Newark, was the man who looked at his watch. Something of a precisionist, he was going for broke, regardless. Alexander had flattened behind a tree with a 10-inch trunk; from it he could see the machine-gun bunker clearly, though the slope between was overgrown with elephant grass for 20 meters or so. He was hoping, as do all riflemen, that the timber would somehow save him, though he did not cower behind it. In the 10 minutes, he emptied 10 magazines (180 to 200 rounds) of M-16 ammo, firing at the bunker. And it was aimed fire; he followed what the trainers had told him. This was his first fight, and he felt great satisfaction that he could do his part, without sweating too much about it.

In the ruck with Second Squad, which had gone flat when the shooting started without really knowing whether the danger was real, was Pfc. Tommy Jones, a hardnosed 20-year-old from Taft, Calif. At his elbow was Private Weight, with Spec. 4 Thomas Tobey of Hartford on his other side. Tobey was a gunner, Weight his assistant, and Jones the ammo bearer.

The least of the three got them in motion. "That's a lot of shooting," Jones said. "We ought to get up there."

"Shouldn't we wait for orders from the lieutenant?" Tobey replied.

Jones bit it off: "You can't win that way."

So they went.

Crawling, they made it, and set up their M-60 about 15 meters to the left of the first machine gun, where Wysocki lay. But the grass was so thick that they could not see him or the weapon.

The gun was still firing as they settled. Then it stopped. From its direction rose an anguished cry, "Medic, medic, medic."

"Someone's gotta take over that gun," Jones said matter-of-factly.

The two gunners didn't reply; they were busy with their own weapons.

So Jones crawled off through the grass on his last do-it-yourself mission. He found Peak and Wysocki down, both hit by bullets.

Tobey and Weight heard the other M-60 machine gun resume its comforting rat-tat-tat. Jones called back to them, "I got it going." By their count, he was a full-fledged gunner long enough to fire at least 200 rounds. Then five bullets hit him all at once, two in the brain, one through the neck, and two in the upper body. It was the hardest possible way to win a Silver Star.

Weight and Tobey guessed that Jones had died when they heard the gun stop a second time. But they were preoccupied with problems of their own. Weight was mystified. He could see the three bunkers, but could not determine which one based the machine gun, and he couldn't see a Charlie anywhere. "Shit, we're fighting ghosts," he said. Tobey replied, "Keep shooting." Tobey seemed to be doing all right with the M-60 on his own, so Weight opened fire with his rifle. Together they put about 700 rounds into the bunker line, 500 of them from the machine gun Tobey was working.

Specialist 4 Rickey D. Barnett, 19, of Santa Ana, Calif., had heard a faint cry, "Jones is hit." Barnett, an aid man, crawled forward through the elephant grass looking for Jones and was astonished to find him dead. But he had too little time to dwell on that. Machine-gun fire ranged in on him and he was pinned flat. He could hear Mumma crying, "Medic, medic." Mumma was not more than five feet from him, but the distance seemed infinite. If he tried to get to Mumma, he would die. So Barnett decided to back away on his belly and picked out a line where three trees grew one behind the other as promising the best chance of making it. He had noted that the M-60 was still in working order, but firing a machine gun was not his task. That put it up to another soldier, and he was not a machine gunner, either. Barnett got back to the dead space he had occupied and crouched down again, reprieved.

Odell's entry into the fire exchange had also been on a volunteer basis. Being Lieutenant Enari's radio telephone operator, he could have played it somewhat safer. Still, the lieutenant was no man to hold back. Early in the action, he had tried to get up to the machine gun. A bullet got him in the leg and decked him. That was coincidental with Peak's wounding.

Odell lay there with him for a minute or so, then realizing that Enari was immobilized and doing no real good, he asked, "Can't I get up there with the guys on line? They're hurting real bad. I can turn the RT over to Private Miller."

Enari thought a moment and said, "OK."

Odell crawled through the grass to Weight's position. Deep in grass, and seeing no one, he sang out, "Is there anybody out in front of me?"

He heard Peak reply. "No one I know about," and recognized the voice.

Odell crawled forward another 10 meters or so, going obliquely to the right, which put him ahead of both machine guns.

"Wysocki, bring your gun up," he called back.

At first there was no answer.

He called again.

Then he heard Wysocki's feeble reply: "I can't. I been hit in the head."

"Tobey, bring your gun up here." Odell called out again. "The cover's better. I want to help Wysocki."

Tobey started. Odell doubled back through the grass to Wysocki. He found him lying flat. Face downward. There was a bullet hole in the back of his head and blood was flowing from his right ear.

"Oh, God no," Odell murmured.

Without looking up, Wysocki said, "I guess I'm on my way out."

"We'll have to see," Odell replied. "But don't get so scared until you really know."

In these moments Odell realized, to his amazement, that he was quite at ease on a battlefield. This product of Manchester Tech is handsome, crew-cut, rather soft-spoken—the all-American boy.

He dragged Wysocki through the grass to behind a young banyan tree, removed his steel pot, and had a good look. What he saw made him whistle.

"You're the luckiest man alive," Odell told Wysocki. "That's only a scratch, a band-aid wound."

Perking up at once, Wysocki said, "Then bring me the gun and I'll get going again."

Enari, the first numbing shock of his bullet wound having passed, dragged himself forward on his belly to within 10 meters of their position behind the tree. He called out to Odell and the others, "Those Charlies are in the trees. Use grazing fire against the bunkers but also fan the trees."

This they did, and they kept it up for 10 minutes or so, with no one else getting hurt.

Enari crawled on up, tapped Odell on the shoulder, saying, "Cease fire, and call it out to the others."

The lieutenant wanted a lull to test the measure of resistance, and, besides, he was worried that his men were running low on ammunition.

After Odell put out the order, Enari crawled back to his old position. Only then did Odell and Wysocki waken to the fact that they had less than 50 bullets left for the M-60 and their one M-16. "We're almost out of ammo," Odell called back to Enari.

Enari propped on one elbow to fling them a bandolier. He didn't make it; another bullet got him in the same leg. He spun about, his body jackknifing. "I'm hit, I'm hit," he cried loudly.

Then another bullet drilled him through the right side of his chest.

"Medic, medic, medic," Enari called out.

But there were no aid men available; the only two that were forward were working on other cases. So Enari crawled to the rear to seek first aid and find it. Eternally surprising are the resources of physical strength a badly wounded man may find when he knows that he must move or will probably die.

The fight had been going at that point for about 45 minutes; it was approximately 0945. Throughout all this time the main body of the company had been in the grip of phantasmagoria, hexed by the mistakes in deployment that had preceded the fire bath given the one squad that was forward, and, in consequence, fighting at white heat against a foe that was never there.

The early order given First Platoon had brought about a twisting of the formation so that it had become shaped roughly in a rectangular perimeter, not unlike a British Square.

Lieutenant Weindel of First Platoon, sent on his wild goose chase, had had time only to send this message to Quann: "I can't find that damn tunnel. I can't find it, anywhere."

Lieutenant Gipson heard the words over the RT. Precisely at that moment the first fire broke against Enari's frontward squad. When it happened, the two strung-out platoon columns forming the flanks and the headquarters element forming the rear of the box became hallucinated. They could not see one another or get any feeling of their situation; hence, the simplest element of control was lacking. Automatically, the men went flat. As they did so, almost as automatically they began firing outward. This noise, this tumult on all sides, created the illusion that swiftly became a fixation.

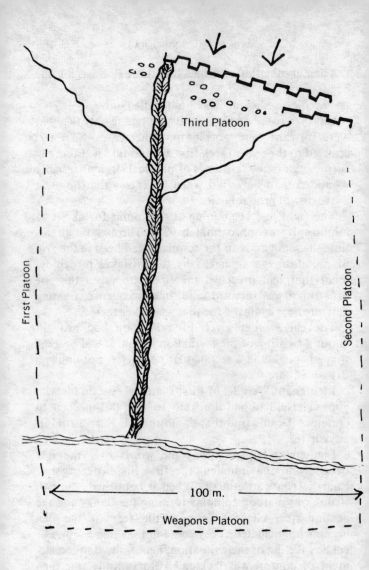

First Platoon

Third Platoon

Second Platoon

← 100 m. →

Weapons Platoon

Company A's deployment. Arrows point to fortified enemy position. U.S. forces thought they were surrounded because of noise created by their own firing.

The troops believed that they were surrounded on all sides by an oncoming enemy and they responded with desperation. So for the greater part of an hour there was a great wastage of ammunition that, far from accomplishing anything, denied Enari's men of needed support and all but doomed them.

It is a spectacle sad beyond imagining. Every move was wrong, though the way each move was made in the assumed situation was exactly right. No one had touched the panic button: a mistake had been made because of misunderstanding, and, once the error was committed, misunderstanding intensified. Quann, being at the center of the noise, was the man least likely to grasp the reality. He was calm and collected as on his big night in September, but sangfroid is no substitute for correct information.

Thirty minutes after the action started Enari had called Quann on the RT, saying, "Give me some artillery." Within three minutes the shells were falling accurately on the NVA base camp.

"How's it doing?" Quann asked.

"Good," Enari replied. "Keep it coming."

Then the gunfire tapered off. At last it stopped altogether, and nobody ever found out why.

"For God's sake," Enari radioed Gipson, "send me some people up here."

"I can't send much," Gipson replied. "We're surrounded and fighting everywhere. I can spare you just one squad."

Enari accepted what Gipson told him as fact. He had no way of knowing that the company was engaging phantoms and only shooting up the countryside.

Specialist 4 Robert J. Winter, a 21-year-old machine gunner from Sauk Centre, Minn., led forward the Third Squad from Gipson's platoon. Advancing, it crossed a gully. A low-hanging tree branch caught in the steel pot of Spec. 4 Martin Barbusa and jerked it off. As he reached for it, a bullet drilled him through the head; the helmet might have saved him. When he dropped, the others continued on.

Sergeant Berned Manzares, squad leader, asked Enari, "Where do you want my people?" Enari motioned him to spread them out along the right flank. They had come up through heavy fire and the fire persisted. With this group was a machine gunner, Pfc. Charles E. Caldwell, 25, of Buffalo. No one told him where to put his gun, so he dropped it behind a small knob and began firing along a trail. He figured "there's a chance someone might come that way."

Enari noted that the North Vietnamese in the base camp appeared to be extending more and more toward his own right, in the direction from which Bravo Company was now coming on. Its columns were at this moment about 800 meters distant and its men could hear the sounds of fire ahead. Lt. Edwin A. Ackerman, 25, of Rochester, Minn., commanding the lead platoon, was urging them on. "We got to rush it," he kept shouting. "They need help." His men moved at a trot, where the ground permitted.

Within 10 minutes, Manzares had felt enough of the fire to realize that at last he was at grips with the real situation. He called Gipson saying, "You must send more men up here."

"We're still surrounded," Gipson told him, "but I'll peel off one fire team from the First Squad."

The fight had been going for more than one hour with no lessening of the illusion.

Manzares called Gipson again. "You must send an aid man up here for our people and for Enari's," he said, then added, "and more people to fight. Here's where the fight is." And there, also, was the one man who saw the situation clearly.

The artillery, called "good," was coming again, but much too close. Private First Class Alexander had taken in his right hand one shard that ripped it open. In about the same moment, Specialist 4 Stewart was hit by an enemy bullet in the right foot; it scraped the ankle and broke his little toe. Then Sgt. Reyes Cruz, a Puerto Rican, was downed by a shell frag in the right leg, and Spec. 4 James Brown was creased by a bullet in the back of the neck. All these casualties were out of Third Platoon.

Sergeant Morris got Quann on the RT. "Now that the artillery is coming, it's wrecking us," he said. "Get it off our neck." The adjustment was made; the fire thereafter pounded the base camp.

Manzares called Gipson another time, saying, "We must have more men. This is the hot spot."

Still convinced that the entire company was enveloped, Gipson nonetheless decided to move up one more fire team. Lieutenant Eastwood of First Platoon protested. "We can't risk it," he said. "You're opening a big hole in an engaged line."

Gipson let the fire team go on. But, taking Eastwood's warning seriously, he also put five engineers and three Vietnamese from a psychological warfare team into the gap where the half-squad had been. The time was then about 1040, and the long-lasting nightmare had all but run its course.

Sudden suspicion dawned on Gipson about then. Despite all the shooting, no one was getting hit around him. Yet casualties kept mounting where he had sent his detachments. Was it all fantasy? He went to Quann and said, "We must get up to Enari's platoon. That's the only way we'll know." Quann nodded in agreement and they went along.

They found Enari in the same gully where Barbusa had taken his bullet. He was down, in great pain, and Specialist Barnett was working on him.

"I been hit bad," Enari said. "So is the platoon. Will you get up there and see what you can do for my men?"

In that moment the light dawned on his two fellow officers. Whether or not it was Enari's agonized earnestness that did it, the bubble broke. Without saying a word, Quann turned about and returned to the other platoons. He knew now that his job was to get people up to help Enari's remnants, and he brooded on his own miscalculations as he walked, kicking himself all the way.

Gipson continued forward on a somewhat zigzag course, not knowing exactly where the fighting line was and having no one to guide him. After rambling about, he got to Sergeant Morris, who hastily outlined his dispositions. "What do you think of it?" Morris asked.

"I think everything you've done is exactly right," the lieutenant said.

Thereafter, Gipson was fully occupied, deploying some of the upcoming hands into the more obvious gaps in Morris' line and teaming the others to evacuate casualties. Weapons Platoon came forward and was deployed as a whole. The engineers and Vietnamese, who had uselessly played the role of the small Dutch boy at the dike, were diverted to hack out a landing zone for choppers so that the wounded could be evacuated.

The time was 1100. The day remained beautifully clear and a hot sun beat down. The temperature was 89. There were already Hueys in the air above them. An air strike had come in, rocketed and bombed the base camp during three passes, then disappeared into the distance.

Due to these interventions, the artillery had to cease fire. When the guns quit, fire came from the enemy camp in the heaviest volume of the day. It happened at exactly the wrong moment, just as Bravo Company hove in sight.

Bravo had gone through misery in closing, not because of the fire but due to finding itself in the same maze of stream beds that had flummoxed Alpha Company. Ackerman, commanding the lead platoon, just couldn't get it. Already on Alpha Company's net, he called Gipson to ask, "How the hell do I find where you are?"

"You will come to a stream about 15 meters wide with straight banks about 10 feet high and running muddy water," Gipson answered. "Follow it along going upstream and you will come in on us."

Ackerman passed the word along to S.Sgt. James Hafford, 31, a hardy and hefty regular from Tacoma, who was in charge of the point. The sergeant took off with his men and, after conning three different creeks, he called Ackerman on the RT to say, "Nuts, lieutenant. We can't do it that way. There are too many creeks. Either we guide on the sounds of the firing or we get lost."

But the fire-fight sounds stayed highly elusive, affording little guidance. After more meandering, Hafford decided to try shouting. His men yelled in the nick of time. Out of sight, on the other side of a small rise, Third Squad, Second Platoon of Alpha Company, was within a stone's throw of them and shouted back.

From atop the rise, Hafford looked back, saw the forefront of Second Platoon on his own side of the last creek, and mistakenly concluded that the entire company was in position to complete the linkup safely.

Just then, Lt. Melvin E. Case, Bravo's commander, heard on his RT from Quann: "We could use one of your squads to help evacuate our people." He followed up with directions. Case was still on the far side of the stream. He said to Spec. 4 Ralph Price, "Take your squad, go to the creek bank, follow it along to the left, and you'll come to the spot where you can help with the evacuation."

As Price took off with his men, S.Sgt. Richard Channell brought his squad of Second Platoon across the stream to join Hafford.

The others, under Lt. Robert E. Pearson, started to cross. Hafford was listening on the radio. Suddenly he heard Pearson's voice break in on Alpha Company's freak, saying, "Hell, we're under fire!"

To begin, it was unimportant, only a few rounds, intermittent shooting from hidden snipers, all of it badly aimed. Here is what had happened, as Gipson saw and reported. On the heels of the air strike, for the first time Quann's men up front saw Charlies, quite a few of them. They were in the clear and running, on an angle leftward from the base camp. It didn't have the look of a charge and Gipson concluded that they were running to clear away from the base before the artillery resumed bombardment. Their line of flight—it was simply an attempt to escape—aimed straight at the angle where Bravo Company, in column, was advancing on Alpha Company's right flank.

A tactical accident? Maybe. Ackerman and the others could not see these skirmishers coming on, and initially there was little alarm because the shooting was so wild. Due to the confusion caused by the streams, Pearson's platoon, unwittingly leapfrogging Ackerman's, had linked up first. Now Ackerman was ordered by Case to advance his platoon obliquely to fill in the ground between Second Platoon and the ground where Alpha Company had the fire fight going. This put him on a collision course with the Vietnamese who were moving out.

In charge of the point squad for Ackerman was S.Sgt. George M. Chambers, a robust 19-year-old from Wilmington, Del. Without incident, the squad got as far as the big gully in which Enari lay, some distance to their left. There they hit the hornet's nest and all control was lost.

At least a half-dozen Charlies lay in skirmish order atop the far side of the gully as the point men started their descent. The first few warning shots went way high; though the crackling of weapons sounded at hand, the men kept moving.

The fire that followed was dead-on. The first scout, Pfc. John Barelli, was hit in the head and took two bullets in the chest, but managed to survive. The second man, Spec. 4 Larry Campos, took two bullets in the chest, dying the following morning. The third man, Pfc. Monnett Gilbey, was shot through the heart. Still, these Americans had not met their fate lying down. In their last moments, they had tried to charge the enemy.

Chambers, moving along at the rear of his squad, hadn't seen the men fall. But bullets were buzzing around him, and he had gone flat. Sgt. Paul Pride, on the brow of the gully, was also hugging dirt. The one man between them, Pfc. Horace Lucas, pushed on up to see what Pride was staring at so fixedly. As he flattened beside Pride, a bullet got him through the shoulders and he slumped over.

"You two up there, start using your weapons!" Chambers called out.

"Weapons, hell," Pride replied. "Everybody up here is either dead or wounded."

All of this took less than a minute; it was Chambers' first knowledge that his squad was all but wiped out.

On a dead run, Chambers sprinted for where the two men lay to take a look, disregarding a shout from Lucas: "Stay back where you are!" While he gazed in stupefaction, wondering about his next move, Lieutenant Ackerman, who was in another and much shallower gully 40 meters to the rear, called, "Bring your squad on back!"

"I can't do it," Chambers yelled back. "I got wounded and dead up here and I don't know how many."

"I say move!" Ackerman insisted.

Chambers crawled on back to him, with a piece of advice: "You better take all the rest of the platoon, moving along the far bank of the gully from the left flank, and try to wipe out that nest of snipers."

About then, Hafford came up. On the net, he had heard Ackerman talking to Case, telling him about the casualties forward in his sector. Hafford, all this time, had been trying to find his platoon.

Hafford asked Chambers, "Where are your casualties?" Chambers described the ground where they lay. Together, they devised a plan. Eight men, with Chambers and Hafford leading a team apiece, would pour out fire from the nigh bank of the gully. Two men, Spec. 4 Tom Nations, a medic, and an RTO, Spec. 4 Bruce Pealer, would work along the floor of the gully from the left and try to bring the casualties out. The fire base got going; Pealer and Nations made a cautious approach. It was unnecessary. By the time they reached the bodies, the Charlies were either dead or fled. The dustoff chopper had Barelli and Lucas on their way out to a hospital in the next 10 minutes.

Gipson had been ordered by Quann to cease fire, lest

by turning weapons against the Viets who were getting away he would down some of Ackerman's men who were moving on the same line in the opposite direction. When his front quieted, Gipson saw large numbers of the enemy pick up and go on the run to the westward. The trouble with this was that once Gipson's men desisted, no one else was on the right ground to bring fire to bear on the targets.

After Bravo Company got up on line, the fire fight continued for another half hour. But it was pretty much one way. The enemy had left behind only a thin, covering rear guard to fight a delaying action. Only sporadic rifle fire came from the base camp; most of the enemy battalion, that is, its survivors, had legged it to temporary safety. But while the fight was white hot, the men with Gipson and Morris had been spread out over a 200-meter front, and all parts of the line were drawing fire.

By 1230 it was mostly over. The two companies then marked time for about three-quarters of an hour, tidying up, eating, resting. A regrouping took place, with squads being tightened to insure control. Both companies moved out with platoons in line, going straight for the base camp, through it, then to the crest of the ridge that lay 200 meters beyond.

The mop-up was anticlimactic. Bunkers and foxholes within the base camp were prodded and prowled as the men moved. A few bullets came against them, so they did not try to rush it. Only one American was wounded, S. Sgt. Raymond Marler, who got a slug through his left shoulder that lodged in his back. Marler was from Gipson's group. "That's my second Purple Heart for the day," he said, grinning. It was first notice to the others that he was a walking, fighting casualty; during the artillery misfire he had taken a frag in the back and bled so little that he didn't call on first aid.

During their search, the men found only 16 enemy dead, though a larger body count was reported later, which the conditions of the fight say must have been nearer the truth than the figure of 16, unless the Charlies are immune to bombs, rockets, artillery fire, and napalm. Two NVA soldiers were captured while dying; to the last, they still worked their weapons, though erratically. There were no prisoners otherwise. The total of weapons captured was 11, and all were AK-47 rifles or SKS carbines. The enemy were no less skilled at extracting machine guns for the retreat than in spiriting away the bodies of their dead.

The threshout was completed not long before dusk. That night, during bivouac, eight of Alpha Company's men, four of them wounded, came down with malaria, additional casualties of the fight. They might have escaped it but for the exertions of the day; exhaustion, more than all else, gives the disease a breakthrough.

Alpha Company had marched out late that afternoon, and its sick men were evacuated from another spot. Bravo Company stayed with the battlefield and had further adventures the next day. For the sticklers of history, who are also interested in the fine points of geography, the fight that day was at coordinates YA-580-540. And it does not need a critic to add that it was from first to last a rather messy affair, redeemed by numerous gleamings of courage, some wasted, some not.

Ordeal by Ambush————

Such were the animal problems burdening and haunting Charley Company, First Battalion, 5th Cavalry, on the evening of 20 November, 1966, that the men talked of little else during the unhappy hour between setting up a perimeter and the establishing of listening posts for night defense just before the dark came quickly.

They had pulled up less than 700 yards from the Cambodian border. The day had been quiet, the weather salubrious, and the early evening promised that the night would bring nothing more untoward than the monotony of their daytime fruitless search. But quiet was not quite the word for the camp. Men talked loudly, too loudly; some whistled and others sang a bit. Spirits were a little too high, though for no good reason, except the natural ebullience of American soldiers after long-seeking of the enemy without finding him.

The time was 1700. Spec. 4 Sonny Robert Cowan, a 19-year-old from Magnum, Okla., was gently kidding Pfc. Willy Stevens, a machine gunner. Willy was working to get his weapon set just right and as he wished it. At that moment a brightly plumed bird came to perch on the branch of a scrub tree a few feet above his head.

"Look at that!" said Willy. "It's a parrot."

Sonny looked. "I'll be damned," he said. "That bird has a banded leg."

Before Willy could reply, the parrot took off, flying straight for Cambodia.

"Do you think I better call in and tell them what we saw?" Sonny asked. "It might involve security."

"Man, man, you're way off base," said Willy. "Parrots can talk but they don't know anything. Maybe they could do better if you crossed them with carrier pigeons."

Feeling very foolish, Sonny decided not to make the call.

However, the problem of the sick scout dog could not be as readily resolved. The company was plain stuck with him. The faithful of a C.I.D.G. outfit, now ailing from some malady that only a veterinarian could understand, he had been taken over by the cavalrymen late in the day only so that he might be evacuated for medical care as soon as possible. The S.P.C.A. should therefore note that kindness to dumb animals is the rule with U.S. soldiers in Vietnam, despite a general impression that kindness is a forgotten word over there.

Except for the sick dog, and Specialist 4 Hummel, who seemed to be suffering from a kidney ailment, the unit, apart from a chronic case of the gripes, was in normal health. Out of compassion for these two, with an eye especially to the scout dog, the decision was made early, at company level. The two invalids would be helped out to the nearest landing zone early on the following morning, escorted by at least one squad of armed men. The platoon to which the squad belonged would stay anchored to the position held during the night until the escort party returned, irrespective of the further movements of the company.

The humanity of this decision is beyond contest. Its practicality and its common sense need not be called into question here. Suffice to ponder all that came of it.

For the First Battalion of the 5th, under command of Lt. Col. Robert H. Siegrist, there had been much beating through the bush during recent weeks, with little accomplished and little blood drawn. The companies had been in the field for 72 days running. Even so, they were in fairly good shape, though the campaigning had reduced average strength to 112 to 115 men per company because of losses from malaria, heat stroke, and accidents. It was only after they were lifted to the Cambodian border in mid-November that replacements were flown to them to lift average strength to 150 men per company. As to balance, the three companies were formed of unseasoned soldiers.

Their earlier missions are not a proper part of this chronicle. The companies experienced ordeal without success, doing things more difficult than dangerous. Finally, they were fielded far to the west in the Central Highlands when special agents reported that three large enemy groups, counting about 2,000 NVA each, were pushing into the region out of Cambodia. Montagnard runners brought the word to the advanced U.S. base at Landing Zone Oasis.

On 17 November, Colonel Siegrist was given a new task: the battalion would conduct an S & D (search-and-destroy operation) for three days along the Ia Drang Valley and into the Chu Pong foothills. So, following the alarm, there were numerous excursions, all leading to little or nothing. Out of 10 or so airborne assaults, all done with pace and much gusto, the battalion remained sans body count, sans war trophies, sans blood trails, sans hopeful signs, sans everything save the will to keep trying.

Siegrist was beginning to think that his luck had run out, and in this he was doubtless right. Then age 43, a resident of Reseda, Calif., and graduate of the University of Maryland, Siegrist years ago started his Army life by enlisting out of the Citadel. A tall and somewhat bulky soldier, saturnine of countenance, Siegrist is low-voiced, deeply reflective, and very much on the solemn side. The habit of command has left his mouth tight and a little sad. But he has a way with troops; men respond to him warmly.

On 20 November there was a change for better or worse, according to the point of view, and Siegrist began feeling like a miner when he sees the bright glint of soft metal in the sands of a creek. The forward air controller, Capt. Earl C. Mizell of Bogalusa, La., reported observing 20 North Vietnamese soldiers in movement between LZ Hawk, a two-ship pad about two miles east of the Cambodian border, and the village of Ph Athena, not more than a stone's throw west of the line. In the light of subsequent events, it is altogether probable that this enemy group deliberately exposed itself and was playing a come-on game. An air strike was laid on the spot where the FAC had sighted the enemy, coming in so much later that, naturally, the quarry was no longer there. Then Charley Company was lifted by Hueys to beat the bushes all through the afternoon well to the west of LZ Hawk; it was a completely futile search that turned up nothing worth reporting. Furthermore, the company had operated with its platoons widely separated, each from the others, and had paid no penalty for so doing, though his prowling went on within mortar range of Cambodia.

That night Charley Company went into perimeter defense north of the Cambodian village of Ph Athena, 700 meters west of the frontier. Seated on low ground, next to a creek bed, the foxholes only partly concealed by low bushes here and there, the position was hardly desirable. Directly to the south of it there was a high smooth ridge, topped with elephant grass, which afforded unlimited observation by the NVA. West of the ridge was a grass-grown flat. A well-marked trail led off directly south from the perimeter, running between the hill and the flat. Just off the trail and to west of it, about 200 meters south of the bivouac ground, were several smaller hills.

As night fell each platoon of Charley Company rigged an ambush position about 100 meters to its front, five men in each party. Near midnight an NVA patrol was intercepted while crawling through the grass toward Third Platoon's ambush. One of the prowlers was killed. This was the first contact, but no soldier at the position felt very good about it. The night was too filled with weird noises.

Early next morning Siegrist prepared to turn part of his battalion toward a new mission. His force had been requested to collaborate with the C.I.D.G. company at Du Co that was bound for a village 13 klicks to the eastward, where it hoped to bag a psychological warfare team from the North Vietnamese Army said to be skulking in the area.

Siegrist was in the act of launching this tangential enterprise when, at 0945, he got a radio message from Charley Company's skipper, Capt. Harold Wunsch: "I have just sighted five of the enemy to our southwest about 200 meters."

That was all. It sounded quite unpromising. The distance would place the five NVA only a hop-skip-and-jump from the Cambodian sanctuary.

Captain Wunsch split his command that morning, and so doing increased the odds against getting away with it twice. The NVA had been given 24 hours in which to observe how the company deployed and to work out an entrapment plan. Inasmuch as the camp was on low ground in sight of the border, and there were hills about, the opportunity was there. Moreover, the patrol that had slipped out of Third Platoon's ambush, losing only one man, should have carried the word, as, in retrospect, it seems likely that the company had been stalked during the first day.

Soon after breakfast, First Platoon was sent packing. It would prowl the countryside far to the southward, marching roughly parallel to the border to search out a heavily forested draw to the southeast. No lift or landing zone was available to insure its return in a hurry.

Third Platoon was anchored to the ground where the night camp had been; it must await the going forth and return of the doggie detail. There was little griping about that; the soldiers would get at least three extra hours lazing about.

Exactly at 0900 Second Platoon and the headquarters group broke camp and started their march along the trail running roughly south-southwest through wide-open country. They safely passed the small hills directly west of the trail and emerged onto the flat, elephant-grass-covered swale. About 125 meters to the west within the grassed plain was a knoll approximately 100 feet long that stood clear 12 feet above the elephant grass.

A small party, the column nonetheless went well-loaded. Each rifleman had 20 magazines for his M-16, two frag and two smoke grenades. There were 1,200

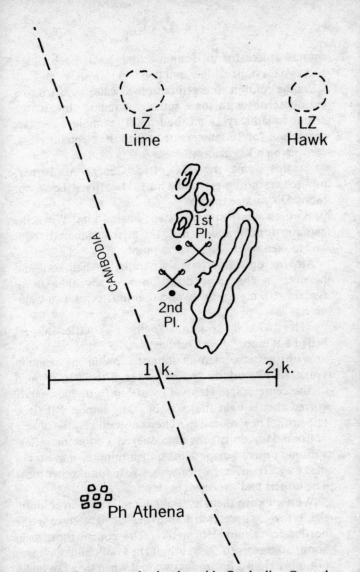

The ambush next to the border with Cambodia. Crossed swords mark sites of ambushes involving First and Second Platoons. LZ's Lime and Hawk are to north.

rounds apiece for all four machine guns. Each squad had two claymore mines and two trip flares.

As the column emerged onto the swale, it shifted to a platoon front with three squads marching abreast, the center squad staying on the trail. They maintained this formation for 100 meters or so into the elephant grass, moving on a 185 azimuth.

At this point, an RTO, Pfc. George A. Turner, pointed an arm westward and said softly, "Look out there. Do you see them?"

Wunsch was just a few steps behind him. When the captain stopped and turned, the men all squared about and looked where Turner was pointing.

Moving on a line roughly parallel to their own and heading in the same direction were five khaki-clad figures, 300 meters away and that much closer to Cambodia.

"Hey, what do you know," Spec. 4 Charles Burgess yelled out loud. "Five Charlies!"

With that, the men all squatted low in the elephant grass. As he sank down, the leader of the Third Squad in the center, Sgt. Henry Lee of Sanford, Fla., wryly voiced the thought that was in many minds: "It's too late now. They've seen us. They know all about us."

In ducking down, the men obeyed a common reflex, without order. For perhaps half a minute, they stayed that way. Then, one by one, they rose for another look. The targets had vanished.

Wunsch gave them a "Follow me!" and, in column, they filed out westward, moving straight toward the border for about 250 meters. The course took them about 50 meters to the south of the knoll, and they were not more than a few rods beyond it when they ran into a speed trail, its dust thickly marked with sandal and boot prints, that ran straight west to Cambodia.

Just about then Wunsch pulled up. Nothing more had been seen of the five figures, and he feared that if he moved on he might, by mistake, violate the frontier. So to close out the prowl in that direction, Wunsch called on the guns to work over the ground westward of him, though he saw no real targets. This is pretty much SOP. Gunners are always happy to oblige and in this instance the somewhat profligate support was provided by B/1/27th, based on LZ Fatima. The fruitless detour toward Cambodia killed about an hour.

At 0945 Siegrist got a message from Wunsch: "We saw them escape across the border," which was a slight exaggeration. The battalion commander was still looking for landing zones closer to the breakoff point that is called the Mantes Line. Within these same minutes he got word that a likely spot had been found the evening before only 1,100 meters directly north of where Charley Company was then moving. He dubbed it LZ Lime and ordered Alpha Company to get there as quickly as possible. By 1000, the support company had closed.

Wunsch and the Second Platoon backtracked the way they had come and, without incident, reached the spot where they had pivoted. That took them past the knoll again. Their backs were now turned to it and they were in the act of wheeling south when Pfc. Jake Van Meter of Slaty Fork, W. Va., chanced to glance back over his right shoulder.

There in clear silhouette standing on top of the knoll were six more NVA soldiers dressed in camouflage, their backs turned to the Americans. They simply stood there, spaced evenly about five feet apart, inviting targets not more than 100 meters away, looking like something to be raised and lowered from a training butt.

But for Van Meter, the main body might have walked

away from it. He passed the word to S.Sgt. E. Logan of
Baltimore, a Negro, all angles, very lean of face and
gently spoken. He gave Wunsch the news. Once again,
the platoon abruptly reversed direction. This time, as
before, there was no firing at first. Wunsch and the
others had the mistaken impression that they were
catching a careless enemy unaware and could sneak up
on him. The failure to engage under conditions where
the platoon was not fully committed beyond extrication
served only to widen the jaws of the trap.

It was 1005 when Wunsch called Siegrist on the radio
telephone to tell him, "I have sighted NVA to my front.
There are at least two squads and maybe a platoon."
Then Wunsch added, "They have their backs turned to
us. I am going to hit them."

Siegrist said, "Go ahead, if it looks OK."

He rated Wunsch an aggressive and sufficiently careful commander who gave his men confidence. Twenty-
seven years old, a Texas A & M graduate pursuing a
Regular Army career, Wunsch is outwardly self-possessed and inwardly not given to sweating hard when
under pressure. His norm was not to coincide with the
requirements of this particular day. Every break went
against him.

The platoon spread out in line, almost lost to sight in
the deep elephant grass west of the trail. It moved forward 30 meters, which brought the line within 70 meters
of the knoll, without a shot being fired. The human
targets stood there, backs turned, completely immobile.
Sgt. Henry Lee simply marveled that the line's advance
had gone undetected. Neither he nor the others could
grasp the terrible, yet essential, fact: the six enemy soldiers were human lures, deliberately risking their lives to
suck the Americans into the trap. It is a thing almost too
brutal for belief.

At 60 meters the Americans opened fire with their rifles while still walking. Three of the targets dropped, riddled through, paying with their lives for the game. Another fell wounded and screaming.

The platoon moved on for another three strides, with marching fire that was not returned, still hugging the illusion that it was about to mop up an already battered picket post. Then automatic fire broke out all along the top of the knoll with at least 20 weapons speaking, and, in a twinkling, Wunsch's men went sprawling in the neck-high elephant grass. Wunsch got off a message to Siegrist over the RT: "I opened fire. We have killed six to eight of them on the knoll." Then Capt. James P. Taylor heard him add this: "I think we are holding our own."

Wunsch's men were spread out over about 75 meters. Depending on where he landed when he hit the ground, each man had a different impression of the situation, the size of the enemy force, and how the fight was going. Few, however, would have agreed with Wunsch's estimate to Siegrist. There were too many bullets scything the grass overhead and kicking up the red dirt in which they lay. And too many others that didn't miss.

In the first two minutes Sergeant Logan heard six different voices cry, "Medic! Medic!" Sgt. Timothy L. Workman of Ashland, Ky., had the squad on the extreme left flank. He saw more than "a dozen of the enemy raise up and fire at us from the ground to the left of the knoll." Then a squad or so tried to move around his flank and he had trouble facing even a few of his men that way.

Sergeant Lee was in the center. It seemed to him that the enemy fire was coming at him from the front and both flanks, though a rifleman can be wrong about that when the heat is on.

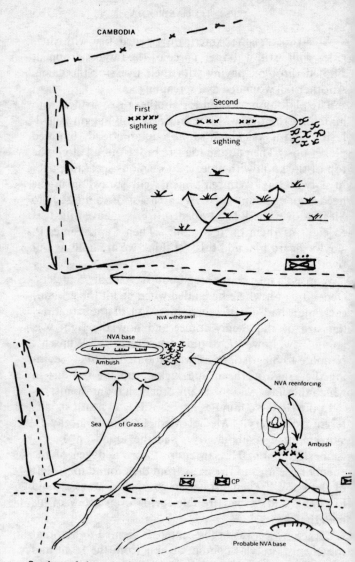

Setting of the two decoys near Ph Athena, top. Arrows show 2nd Platoon's march to border and back. Double ambush and American counterattack, bottom.

Private First Class Edward McCoin of Meadow Bridge, W.Va., flattened out on the far right, had a first impression that the bullets grazing the ground around him were coming only from the enemy right, farthest away from him. But that gave him no comfort, for the whine and drone just above where he had stretched out sounded much too personal to him.

Private First Class Larry M. Williams of Clayton, N.C., fired only six or seven times, then a pin dropped out of his M-16. Unable to find it, he was momentarily weaponless. Sergeant Workman, a friend in need, lay about five meters from him. Williams called to him, "My piece is out."

"See any targets?" Workman asked.

When Williams said "yes," Workman tossed him his own M-16.

Williams fired several times, then on demand threw the rifle back to Workman.

They continued this way, alternately firing, throwing the M-16 back and forth, a game not for children, and hardly recommended for infantry.

"How long can we keep this up?" asked Williams.

"As long as we got to," replied Workman.

Specialist 4 William H. O'Neill Jr. of Fallsburg, N.Y., a machine gunner on the extreme right flank, fired most of his basic load in the first 10 minutes, after crawling almost to the base of the knoll. Here was raw courage, largely unrewarded. The view up front was most unsatisfactory. A cluster of well-leafed saplings obtruded between his sights and the target and he could not be sure that any of the bursts were hitting home. But he was quite certain that he heard no machine gun firing from the knoll. It was all AK-47 rifle fire. An NVA sniper got on his right flank, pinned him down, and put several rounds through the M-60. O'Neill crawled on back through the elephant grass, which was just as well.

Private First Class Vitus Quillet of Clarksville, Ind., the point man for the Second Squad, hand-in-hand with his guardian angel, advanced all of 10 meters beyond the knoll, and was twice that distance to the left of it. From that vantage point he saw five Vietnamese crawling down the slope that he was covering. One was in black pajamas, the others were in camouflage. They were maneuvering to get on the American flank. Quillet blasted them with his M-16. Then he heard a call from Sgt. Frank C. Giordana, who was about 30 meters to his right and rear.

"I got to have machine-gun ammo," said Giordana.

Quillet chanced to be toting two magazines, an odd carry for a rifleman trying to stay mobile under the heat. He crawled to Giordana and delivered them; Giordana grunted, "Much obliged," giving the action one more whiff of courtesy.

But they had all passed the point of no return and were aware of it. Spread out and separated as they were, with few of them mobile and the greater number, if not pinned, then flattened by the fire, it was already impossibly late to order them to back away. And, as for charging forward, it is done, under these conditions, only in the movies.

Wunsch had a morsel of satisfaction. His men were fighting back well enough. The surprise hadn't stunned them. They were responding like Trojans. But weren't they trying a little too hard? Every man seemed to be firing automatic.

He stood erect, preparing to yell out that they should go easy on the ammunition. Twice he called, "Slow that fire!"

From somewhere along the high ground to the rear a sniper cracked down on him, and the first bullet hit him in the right elbow. Wunsch fell, not dangerously wounded, but hard hurt and bleeding badly. Though conscious, he said nothing. Momentarily he seemed stunned. An aid man crawled over to him, slapped a bandage on the wound, and gave him two shots of morphine.

Together, the shock impact of the bullet and the effect of the drug finished Wunsch. He made feeble attempts, but could no longer truly function.

From that time forward the action was split-trail commanded by two soldiers, young Spec. 4 William D. Tuey of Phoenix, Ariz., a white gunner-observer, and Sergeant Logan, a Negro with six years of regular service behind him. The technical half of the job, mainly calling-in and directing the heavy fires, fell to Tuey. Logan rallied and directed the men. It was a natural division of talents, arrived at by mutual consent. They did not consult Wunsch. They simply took over.

That happened just about 15 to 20 minutes after the fight started, almost coincidentally with the upsurge of firing back along the trail where Third Platoon had been left. It was heavy volleying, the whine of bullets rising sharply above the rattle of Second Platoon's own fight.

Wunsch was lying next to his RTO, McCoin. "Call Third Platoon," he said, "and tell them to cut out all of that damned noise." It occurred to McCoin that the captain wasn't thinking very clearly any longer. He didn't send the message. He ignored him for two reasons, neither having anything to do with the message's impropriety. McCoin was scared, and he was firing as fast as he could get the bullets out. Still, he saw Wunsch pick up the RT and say loudly, "Cut out that damned firing over there."

Wunsch's aberration was considerable. He soon was on the RT talking to Siegrist, whose Huey was orbiting above the battlefield: "Third Platoon reports people all around them; they're telling me they're surrounded." A few minutes later, Captain Taylor picked up this message from Wunsch: "The enemy is on at least three sides of Third Platoon, which is getting grenaded." Maybe another five minutes passed before Siegrist got this directly from Wunsch: "I think we probably have lost them."

McCoin was unaware that Wunsch was sending these messages, and neither he nor any other soldier near the captain knew how he had collated the information on which he had based his conclusion.

Tuey, a 20-year-old, has the mien and manner of a man twice his age. Physically a shrimp, both short and slight, with a spare, rigidly set face that never cracks a smile, he is dour to the extreme. His words are so crisp that they sizzle. Polity isn't in him. He is a superb fighter who is at his best when the pressure breaks other men. This morning, he was already burning before one shot had been fired. Emboldened by an instinct that cried warning, he had said to Wunsch, as the column had begun its move south from the night position, "Captain, you are taking this company right into an ambush." It was not his job, really; he was only an acting recon sergeant with Second Platoon. But he doubted Wunsch's judgment altogether. And Wunsch, busy with other thoughts, paid him no attention.

So it was Tuey who got on the radio to Third Platoon and, without asking Wunsch's permission, said, "We're in trouble. Come up fast and help us." That was about 15 minutes after the fight started. Tuey had no knowledge that Third Platoon had been anchored to the night position, waiting for the return of the squad that was walking a sick dog to the LZ. Had he known, he would probably have called anyway, being that kind of man.

Private First Class John Godfrey of Third Platoon took the call. "Just a minute and I'll see," he said. There was a brief break in the conversation. Godfrey came on again after a prolonged silence: "We're on our way."

Tuey put up the phone. In another minute Godfrey radioed, "We're not moving and I don't know why." Another long pause followed before Godfrey spoke again: "Looks like we're going into an ambush position back here." They broke off. Another minute and Godfrey called again: "We're getting sniper fire."

Again Third Platoon's spokesman went off the air. Then came the last call from Godfrey: "We're surrounded. For God's sake bring artillery fire in on us!"

Tuey wasted no time cussing or communing with Wunsch. He called Major Johnson instantly. "Give them concentration Uniform Charlie one-eighteen," he said. This was a preset fire to be used against an ambush position. Tuey had also given Johnson the coordinates.

"Look, I can't give you battery three," Johnson replied. "It's too much fire. I'll give you battery one."

"Let it come," Tuey said.

He heard the shells break, and called Godfrey: "How does it look?"

Godfrey gave him a correction.

Tuey put it in to Major Johnson: "Make it a right, drop 200, and give them battery four." So saying, he was bucking a field officer.

This time Johnson raised no question. The shells came on.

Godfrey spoke one more time. "That's good," he said. "Keep it coming."

Then contact between company and Third Platoon was broken for the last time. And Tuey instinctively knew what had happened. "God damn it!" he said aloud. "They're all dead."

Over the radio, he gave it to Johnson: "I figure there's nobody left there."

Johnson said very quietly, "You ask Wunsch if he wants the fire shifted." He could tell from the noise over the PRC that the people fighting against the position on the knoll were now catching hell.

Wunsch said, "Tell him to move the fires to us."

From the small stream bed to the right of the knoll a half-dozen rocket launchers were now banging away at the field where the main body lay flattened. This was danger from a new quarter. McCoin rolled over in the grass to take a new position. Five seconds later a Soviet-made RPG-7 rocket exploded in the spot where he had lain.

Sergeant Lee called to him, "That's a reenforcement. The gooks that got Third Platoon have swung over against us." It was a well-educated guess.

Tuey was listening hard. He could no longer hear any sounds of a fight where Third Platoon had been.

A great part of the rocket shower was hitting into ground between Lee, McCoin, and Pfc. Lyman Beaver, a 20-year-old rifleman from King's Mountain, N.C., who was far over to the right. It didn't stop Beaver. He continued firing with his M-16, both at the stream bed and against the knoll, and in the next hour he exhausted his ammo supply—425 rounds. That's as much as may be asked of any fighter. Yet he, Tuey, Lee, and all the others who employed weapons were having to raise their heads and prop for firing. Otherwise, they could not see either of the main targets, so high was the elephant grass.

• • •

The sudden arrival and pitiless accuracy of the NVA rocket attachment might well have done them all in. It was a shocker. McCoin saw the group with the launchers appear for a moment as they dipped down into the creek to the right of the knoll; they were lost to sight before he could do anything about it. O'Neill, now without a machine gun, saw them also, and too soon was under their fire. Because of the angle of the creek embankment that the enemy was using as a breastwork, the thrust of this fresh assault was mainly against the right flank of Second Platoon's line. Tuey and Logan, who were operating around the command post in the center, had not even a vague impression of how much real damage was being done there. But the noise was deafening.

Not until 1040 did Major Johnson monitor a call from Tuey: "We request medevac." The fight had been going more than a half hour; it was the first signal to the rear echelons that Charley Company was being hurt.

Third Platoon had been dead for at least 25 minutes, with Second Platoon fully engaged for twice that long when Tuey again got through to Johnson to ask for help from rocket ships, or any other air that could beat down the batteries in the creek. "I want you to put marking rockets out first, 100 meters on either flank, then drop the stuff about 75 meters in front of us," Tuey said. Johnson passed the word along from his CP, but it was 1130 before the air became alerted; and the ships were still far away.

The strikes finally came in between 1205 and 1235. Through this time, Siegrist was in his command ship above the battlefield, From his height he could not judge the effect of the strikes, but, then, he had only a vague idea of what Second Platoon was up against, though he already guessed that Third Platoon had been wiped out.

Tuey, anxiously awaiting the strikes, felt distress and disappointment after they were delivered. It wasn't enough. "There were only two gunships. They made a couple of passes, dropped half a load and dropped it in the wrong place." It is not uncommon for the ground fighter, sweating it out and preoccupied with his own problem, to downrate what the air may contribute to his deliverance, unless the relief is instant and total.

The facts of the matter, however, are incontrovertible. It was at 1010 that morning that Maj. R. C. Mitchell, the brigade air liaison officer, first heard of the contact, though there was consequently no alert or leaning toward the scene of action by the air. Captain Mizell, the FAC, was aloft in an 0-1 above LZ Oasis when at 1130 he got the first call, this from Major Johnson. He headed for the scene of action. His first information, at 1130, was "light contact." Enroute, this was changed to "heavy contact," an almost two-hour lag in the adjustment of information. He arrived above the fight just as the first two gunships were pulling off. Over his radio, he heard Tuey saying to Siegrist, "They're still within hand-grenade range of us."

Siegrist said to Mizell, "Get air here quick!" There were A-1 jets at Pleiku, 20 to 25 minutes' flight time away. While they were coming on, Mizell got his own fix on Second Platoon's position. Mizell stayed high so that he would not get in the way of the strikes. Although he saw too little, he checked off what was thrown at the knoll in 13 passes altogether: 4,000 pounds of napalm, 10 CBU's, and 3,000 rounds of 20-mm. fire.

Logan watched at close range, and, to Logan's eye, the fight turned on the coming of the A-1's. They broke the back of the NVA resistance. The men flattened in the field saw several figures arise on the knoll, made into torches, their clothing aflame all over. One burning communist was still working his rifle. Later Captain Taylor checked out 10 NVA bodies clustered close together. They carried no wounds. They were not burned. They had died from suffocation.

Throughout the early stage of engagement the detached First Platoon had been slogging south under the command of Lt. Timothy J. McCarthy of Ossining, N.Y. He is a quite deliberate soldier, almost oddly undramatic. The footing was good, the countryside quite open, except for patches of elephant grass, and so the column slipped along rather rapidly, all hands believing that there was little danger from ambush. The mission was simply a straight-away prowl, a poking-about in search of Charlie. By 1000, or a few minutes after the main body became involved, McCarthy was all of 1,700 meters due south of his starting point. The distance was much too great to make mutual support meaningful, but then no tether had been put on McCarthy.

On the stroke of the hour came a call on the PRC-25 from Wunsch. The captain said only, "We have seen some Charlies!"

McCarthy thought he heard the sounds of fire. "Then I think I better come back," he said.

"No," Wunsch replied. "I don't need you."

McCarthy urged him, saying, "You can't be sure."

There was dialogue for several minutes. At last Wunsch said, with some reluctance, "All right, come on back."

McCarthy turned his men about and they started out, at first jogging, a pace quickly dropped because of the heat. Then the column got off course and lost its way and more time. After the slowdown, the men could hear heavy gunfire to the north.

McCarthy got on the radio again. This time he was talking to Sergeant Logan, the Negro, a heads-up veteran and matter-of-fact soldier.

Logan said, "Lieutenant, can't you see those air strikes? You just guide on them. You'll run into us."

McCarthy took a good look. In the far distance he could indeed see, not air strikes exactly, but either gunships or ships of the ARA (aerial rocket artillery) making their runs from east to west. The guidance was being provided by Tuey, with Major Johnson serving as relay and passing the information to the pilots.

"I see ARA," said McCarthy.

"Then come on fast," said Logan.

They picked up the jog again, but quickly dropped it. The strikes had pulled off. The blue sky was now perfectly clear, providing no pillar of fire to guide them by day, and, in the no-landmark sea of grass, getting lost is easier than going straight.

The strike had been anything but overpowering. Two ships had come in, first flying from south to north, but dropping nothing. Then they flew east to west, right over the heads of Wunsch and his men, dropping their napalm loads 40 yards in front of the Americans and a little to the left of the knoll. There were no anti-Dow Chemical Company preachers or undergraduate mobs to stop them.

Logan sighed, "Man, that looks almost good," then turned to Giordana and asked, "Was it good? Did it hit anything?"

"No, but it was pretty close to good," Giordana answered. "Tell them to put some more a little to the right."

There was no one to tell. The two ships, having given their all, had departed for home base.

At that moment, McCarthy was still about 1,000 meters to the south, with Logan sweating out his absence. McCarthy himself figured he was within a quarter mile of the action. Logan again got on the radio, this time to the RTO, Private First Class Bass, asking, "Can't you guide on the sounds of our fire?"

"We ain't hearing nothing," Bass replied.

So Logan threw out red smoke, still thinking that McCarthy's estimate of 250 meters must be about right. Because it wasn't, the grenade was just another wasted one. Logan kept on throwing out red smoke. When McCarthy at last saw it, his column was 200 meters north of the position (having marched too far), and once more he had to backtrack. In this way, much more than an hour was lost.

Coming even with the line on which Wunsch and his men had deployed, McCarthy saw green smoke on one flank, red on the other. Tuey had brought the stuff in there, directing the aircraft. Although McCarthy thought the two plumes marked the outer limits of the American-held ground, he held up for at least five minutes about 100 meters to the rear to get his troops squared away and to be sure of control.

By then the fight was all but over, though there was still the rat-tat-tat of automatic fire, most of it coming from the right side of the enemy-held knoll.

First Platoon crawled forward through the ground held by Second Platoon. On all fours, McCarthy got up to Wunsch and reported.

Wunsch croaked at him, "I don't think we got anyone killed." Surprised only by the rasp in Wunsch's voice, and knowing nothing of the trauma the captain had gone through or about the morphine, McCarthy took the evaluation at face value and felt suddenly good and grateful.

It was time for wisecracking. "Nuts," McCarthy said, "I thought you were in a real fight and here you been resting while we were running our tails off."

Wunsch broke it off. "Go on up there and secure that knoll," he ordered. "I don't think there's anyone left up there."

He didn't tell McCarthy the knoll was where the NVA resistance had come from, or anything else that might have cautioned or rebuked him.

So McCarthy took just four hands with him, Sgt. King A. Smith and Privates First Class Moseley, Kruse, and Bulley. He concluded that his earlier impression about fire still coming from the knoll must have been wrong. In this clutch, his patron saint saved him; the few live NVA skirmishers that had clung there pulled away while he was going forward. Otherwise, he would be dead now.

The five men almost recoiled in shock when, on topping the knoll, they found it littered with brayed flesh, torn limbs, and the bodies of the dead and dying. "Jesus," McCarthy said, "this is terrible. They have been in a real fight."

Other men of the platoon had come forward to check the forward slope; they found mainly bloody bandages and blood trails. At the same time, Sergeant Smith was prodding his mates working the crestline to collect all NVA weapons, of which there was a small arsenal. Though this indicated a hasty departure by the enemy, McCarthy had no intention of pursuing. It was too close to Cambodia, and, besides, he did not yet know the condition of the company. So he tolled off one squad of men to outpost the knoll.

Sickened by the sight and the stench, McCarthy decided to get back to Wunsch, but because he had moved forward via Second Platoon's left flank he decided to return via the right flank of the position to check out things as he moved. What he found stunned him far more than his earlier discovery on top of the knoll. He counted them one at a time—13 dead from his own company. And he still did not know that one entire platoon had been wiped out. So Wunsch had been wrong about it, wrong as a man could be. "My God, oh, my God," McCarthy said to himself.

Each body lay flattened behind a small tree. The four-inch saplings, other than three anthills and the elephant grass, were the only cover on the smooth dirt flat over which they had deployed. McCarthy got on his hands and knees to have a closer look, mystified by the manner of these deaths. McCoin, the compassionate radio operator for Wunsch, that very active soldier, soon joined him, and they moved from body to body. What they noted mainly was that there was a small crater within reach of where each man had died. Some were twice the size of a fist, others were larger.

"I think it was rockets that got them," McCoin said. "Look at those marks."

"No, I don't think so," said McCarthy. "In loose earth, grenades would do that. But a whole pack of Charlies must have worked themselves up close, unseen."

The mystery was never completely solved. Neither man's theory fitted the circumstances. The elephant grass was not more than 18 inches high where these men had died; a sneak grenading of them all, at one time, would have been impossible. No shower of rockets could have worked such perfect execution that not one soldier survived, there amid the saplings.

"It's a rough war," McCoin said, "and I got a hell of a bellyache."

McCarthy nodded. He felt numb all over and momentarily his senses reeled. But he knew that he would not carry the news to Wunsch. He would leave that to someone else. By this time it was high noon and the sun beat down. He lay for a few minutes in the shade of the trees, trying to collect his thoughts.

Logan had taken charge of policing the battlefield, and was directing about two squads of men who were treating and moving the wounded and collecting the dropped weapons. So it fell to the overworked sergeant to check out the KIA's and carry the word to the captain that Second Platoon had suffered a bad day, almost as bad as the Third.

Little Tuey, who by default had virtually commanded the action, with Logan sharing part of the responsibility, had relapsed into his normal role as gunner-observer. He felt bitter as gall about the whole affair, and he kept telling himself, "None of this should have happened."

Throughout this time Colonel Siegrist was doing all that any commander might to help his own people out of heavy trouble. The limitations of remote control made him sweat all the harder. His information was all too scanty; he could guess that something terrible had happened but he did not know what. His imagination might have run riot, had he not reminded himself that first reports from a scene of action are usually to be discounted and things are seldom as grim as they seem.

At LZ Lime, 1,100 meters from the battle scene, Capt. James W. Drake was standing by with 57 men of Alpha Company. Drake, too, only knew of the fight what information he had heard by monitoring the battalion network. Though he didn't think anything was terribly wrong, he knew Wunsch was fighting. For Drake, a thoroughly aggressive soldier, that was more than enough, though he hadn't heard one word from Wunsch. He said over the radio to Siegrist, "I want to move. I've got to move."

"Move then," Siegrist said. "Shag ass and get on down there."

They took off in platoon column—First Platoon, the CP group, Third Platoon—and they tried to double-time wherever the going permitted, which was seldom. Nature bucked them most of the way. The route was densely grown with heavy scrub tangled with creepers and thorn vines that clutched at their clothing. When at last they emerged into the green swale where the ambush had been rigged, a first view charmed them; it was by comparison "like entering upon a city park." Even so, they had run the 1,100 meters in 40 minutes.

Out of caution more than from sheer fatigue, they suddenly slowed, though they were sweated through and shaking from the effort. It was high noon, and they were approaching the small mound-like rise where Third Platoon had made its last stand. They had fanned out in line over a 200-meter front from the hill directly north of the battle area. Moving on that broad front, their flanks extended well beyond the end of the mound of the massacre.

Drake was in the center of the line as they started upslope, moving slowly, still wondering what they would find. Not more than 15 paces along he began to get his answer. A dead American lay there, facedown, his arms extended forward, in his right hand a live frag grenade with the pin pulled, nothing but the pressure of the stiffening thumb forestalling explosion.

Drake yelled to his men, "Get back! Get back!"

He reached down, grabbed the grenade from the dead hand, and threw, all of this in one motion. The missile exploded while still in the air.

From that point on their brief maneuver was only a heart-breaking body count of friends. The corpses were all facedown, and all were pointed in one direction, forward. There were 19 bodies, strung out along the dim trail over a distance of not more than 30 meters. The body of Sgt. Bobbie Leadbetter, the leader, was farthest south, alone, three strides ahead of any of the others. The other bodies were scattered in clumps of three or four behind the spot where he fell. Although all weapons, except one Colt .45, had been taken, personal effects had not been disturbed. There was a wallet with each body. The lead men still wore their steel helmets. The enemy had fled before completing their usual thorough job of collecting the loot.

All the bodies were badly battered and mangled. The look of them gave Drake his first random impression that the mass execution must have been wrought with grenades. Still, it could not have been so. Grenades are never that accurate, and moving men, if beset by grenadiers, would certainly scatter in all directions. The circumstances all said clearly that the platoon was massacred in a few seconds by automatic bullet-firing weapons from behind along the flanks. Thereafter, while the victims lay there, some of them wounded, they were separately grenaded by the North Vietnamese, to finish them off.

Drake and some of his men backtracked about 100 meters over the trail that Third Platoon had come. Enroute, they found other signs, one dead Charlie lying in a creek bed, his rifle missing, then, last, the embers of a fire and, over it, a GI coffee pot, filled, the liquid still warm. It mystified Drake, and is a mystery still. Did it mean that Third Platoon had left its mooring, taken out after the main body, then fallen out for refreshment, while barely started on the journey?

While Drake pondered the question, an aid man came running. "There's one survivor," he reported. "I've found a wounded American."

Coming along behind him was Sgt. Julius Durham of Eltzer, S.C., one of Third Platoon's squad leaders. Durham had taken a bullet through his right arm.

Drake felt a certain sense of embarrassment. He didn't wish to question Durham about how the massacre had occurred, though Durham seemed quite self-possessed. It seemed an impropriety because Durham was from another company. And, besides, Drake felt pressed to push on and get to Wunsch and the real battlefield as quickly as possible. So the last good chance to determine precisely how the enemy had gotten away with it was passed up.

Drake merely asked, "Sergeant, how bad is your wound? And can we do anything for you?"

"I'll be OK," Durham said with dignity. "I'm not hurting too much."

He volunteered no information about the tragedy to which he conceivably was the only American eyewitness. Too soon, he was evacuated out of base camp and on his way back to the United States. Durham could have been hit at the ambush site where Godfrey reported that Third Platoon had pulled up temporarily. He may have missed the spot of the massacre altogether.

Within a few minutes Drake and his 57 men were sweeping toward the knoll where McCarthy's men were hard at their tidying-up task. They had not tarried more than five minutes with Third Platoon's dead and they moved not more than 60 meters beyond Second Platoon's ground in their walk west toward Cambodia. Already the elephant grass stood far higher than Drake's head.

"I don't like it," Drake said out loud. "This is not the place to be."

Just then he got an order from Siegrist over the radio: "You either hold up there, or come on back."

Happy to be told, Drake faced his men about and walked away.

Still, there were other survivors from Third Platoon, witnesses no less to the mystery and menace of the early morning. The men of the walk-the-dog detail, who did not like their task one bit, felt itchy from the beginning and became more aggravated as they moved along.

Sergeant Henry Brown of Harrisburg, Pa., a Negro with 12 years in the Regular Army, their leader, was the most discontented of the lot. Any number of things rankled the old soldier. He had killed a man the night before. Shortly before midnight he had gone on listening-post duty. Quickly, his ear caught the sound of movements in the elephant grass to his front and flanks. He thought at first he was hearing animals. There was no wind. Just a whisper to begin with, a very subdued rustling, the sounds grew louder and more persistent. Then, all of a sudden, they seemed to come straight at Brown with a rush. He fired blindly into the grass just above ground level. Five dark forms sprang up and darted away. But Brown could hear one man left behind, screaming. He dove forward into the grass and grappled till the form went silent. It was a North Vietnamese soldier with an AK-47 rifle, six grenades, a full, new pack, and a nigh spotless khaki uniform. Later, Brown heard more noises of the same sort, enough to convince him that the visitors were numerous.

Yet, when morning came, the company seemed to read no warnings out of the incident. Its noise discipline was execrable. Men shouted back and forth as if they were at base camp. On the other hand, the perimeter, as Brown reckoned things, was bound to be under full observation from the high ground directly south of it; there was nothing to prevent it.

Wunsch and the main body had already hit the trail when, at about 0925, Brown lined up the 13 men of his walk-the-dog patrol charged with delivering the animal and Specialist Hummel to LZ Hawk. Cowan, who had been rattled the evening before by the Cambodian-bound parrot, was in the patrol. So was Pfc. Wesley Harland Polland, a 20-year-old soldier from Hayward, Calif. Polland was the RTO for the patrol.

The two heard Leadbetter tell Brown just before the jumpoff, "When you return, we'll be right here. Wunsch told me to stay in place until you get back."

Brown said somberly, "That doesn't sound like a very smart idea."

Before the patrol was on the road more than 15 minutes, Brown was certain that he had called the shot. He knew that enemy skirmishers had followed him out. Bullets from the rear were clipping the elephant grass round about them. They crouched low and kept going, knowing they were being scouted.

Brown said to Polland, "Raise the company and tell them what's happening to us. They need to know this country is crawling with VC."

But Polland's PRC-25 radio couldn't raise either the company or the platoon, which was one more mischance of the morning.

They were already 500 meters along, about a half hour after the start, when they heard the sounds of heavy firing on their rear.

Brown stopped the patrol. "Try to find out what's happening," he said to Polland.

But Polland could not make it a dialogue. Listening hard, he could only get snatches of the action and he called it out to the others who listened, fascinated, forgetting the stalkers on their own rear.

"It's Godfrey on the RT . . . His voice sounds very excited . . . He says they are drawing sniper fire . . . He says they are being surrounded by VC . . . He says they are up and trying to move again . . . He says Leadbetter has been shot in the back."

That was where Godfrey broke off, and the patrol heard its last from the platoon, with nothing coming from the company. There had been about seven minutes of Polland's running monologue, with the RTO all along quoting Godfrey. So Polland got far more from the man about to die than did Tuey. But so great was the tension of those moments that later members of the patrol could recall only these few of Godfrey's words.

While Polland ticked it off, a few members of the patrol fired at random back over the way they had come. There was no more firing from that direction. The stalkers had faded away.

Cowan asked Brown, "Do you think we better turn back?"

Brown hesitated for just a second before announcing his decision out of dilemma.

"No," he said, "we just keep moving along. Those are my orders."

So the 13 soldiers resumed their march to the east, covering a sick dog and a sick man.

While beyond the knoll, Captain Drake and his company could get no idea about the direction in which the NVA survivors had slipped away. And, in truth, they did not tarry long enough to read such signs as were there. The moment Siegrist gave Drake the green light, Drake said to his men, "We're going to beat it out of here in less than two minutes."

Captain Taylor's company, which had drawn a blank in its morning mission of looking for an enemy psywar team, was lifted into LZ Lime in mid-afternoon. From there, Siegrist at once sent the company on a screening toward the south, beating the bushes in search of the vanished force. Close to the border, and 2,000 meters beyond where he started, Taylor came at last to a trace. It was a track of beaten-down grass; the blades were just beginning to straighten. The track was all of 75 meters wide. Taylor guessed that a battalion must have passed that way. His company of 150 men made no such dent on the scenery; closed up in line, its track was about 40 yards wide. The company followed the trace northwest into Cambodia for 350 meters, at which point Taylor got orders to turn about. So these men had invaded. It was hardly hot pursuit; the enemy was long-gone and the day was fading.

For the blunders of omission and commission responsible for working it into a double ambush, Charley Company paid a terrible price. At day's end it had 19 dead in Third Platoon, and one more man died later, with 14 KIA's and 13 wounded in Second Platoon.

The first reported body count of the enemy was 102, later changed to 144. It is unlikely that either was a gross exaggeration and still more certain that neither was either proved or provable. In this particular, the summing-up was no more hit-or-miss than what was reported of other fought-over fields near Cambodia and elsewhere in the war.

There is a final footnote, the terms in which this sad little fight was reported to the American people by a press bureau in remote Saigon, the words of which follow:

"A hopelessly outnumbered U.S. Army platoon of 21 men stood off a 400-man North Vietnamese battalion for four hours Monday. In the end it called in artillery fire on its own positions as the Communists engulfed it in human wave assaults. Only three Americans survived by playing dead. A platoon usually numbers 44 men but the smaller First Air Cavalry Division unit killed at least 102 Communists before they were overrun."

Such was the brief but glorious epitaph for Third Platoon, which had spent itself so vainly.

Glossary————————————

AA	antiaircraft gun
ADC	assistant division commander
AK-47	standard enemy (automatic) rifle
AO	area of operations
APC	armored personnel carrier
ARA	aerial rocket artillery
C & C	command and control
CBU	cluster bomb unit
Charlie	North Vietnamese, or VC
Chinook	large, cargo-type helicopter
C.I.D.G.	Civilian Irregular Defense Group, a mercenary company in pay of the U.S.
CO	commanding officer
commo	communication wire
CP	command post
dustoff Huey	medical evacuation helicopter
E & E	escape and evasion
FAC	forward air controller
FDC	fire direction center
FO	forward observer (artillery)
freak	radio frequency

G-2	intelligence officer
G-3	operations officer
gunship	armed helicopter
HE	high explosive
hootch	hut
HMG	heavy machine gun
Huey	UH-1 helicopter used for command purposes and carrying squads into battle
Husky	Air Force medical evacuation craft
KIA	killed in action
klick	kilometer
LAW	light antitank weapon, used by infantry
LP	listening post
LZ	landing zone
M-14	7.62-mm. caliber rifle that replaced the M-1
M-16	lightweight, 5.56-mm. caliber rifle adopted by Army especially for war in Vietnam
M-60	standard 7.62-mm. machine gun
M-79	grenade launcher
net	radio network
NVA	North Vietnamese Army
OP	outpost
PRC-25	lightweight infantry field radio
PRC-74	heavy-type infantry field radio
psywar	psychological warfare
Puff the Magic Dragon	C-47 with three 7.62-mm. guns that fire 5,400 rounds a minute
reaction force	relief force
relay Huey	communications helicopter
RPD	enemy light machine gun
RPG-7	Soviet-made enemy rocket

RT	radio telephone
RTO	radio telephone operator
S & D	search and destroy operation
S-2	staff intelligence officer
S-3	staff operations officer
sitrep	situation report
SKS	enemy carbine
slick	unarmed copter used for troop movements
SOI	standing operations instructions
tac	tactical air support
TA-1	sound-powered telephone set
TF	task force
VC	Vietcong
WIA	wounded in action
Yards	Montagnard soldiers

Index————————————————

continued

continued

continued

continued

continued

WAR BOOKS
FROM JOVE

08578-2	**AIR WAR SOUTH ATLANTIC** Jeffrey Ethell and Alfred Price	$3.50
08297-X	**BATAAN: THE MARCH OF DEATH** Stanley L. Falk	$3.50
08477-8	**THE BATTLE OF LEYTE GULF** Edwin P. Hoyt	$3.95
08674-6	**BLOODY WINTER** John M. Waters	$3.95
07294-X	**THE DEVIL'S VIRTUOSOS** David Downing	$2.95
07297-4	**HITLER'S WEREWOLVES** Charles Whiting	$2.95
07134-X	**DAS REICH** Max Hastings	$3.50
08695-9	**THE SECRET OF STALINGRAD** Walter Kerr	$3.50
07427-6	**U-BOATS OFFSHORE** Edwin P. Hoyt	$2.95
08341-0	**THE BATTLE OF THE HUERTGEN FOREST** Charles B. MacDonald	$3.50
08236-8	**WAKE ISLAND** Duane Schultz	$2.95
08887-0	**PATTON'S BEST** Nat Frankel and Larry Smith	$3.50
07393-8	**SIEGFRIED: THE NAZIS' LAST STAND** Charles Whiting	$3.50
09030-1	**A DISTANT CHALLENGE** Edited by Infantry Magazine	$3.50
08054-3	**INFANTRY IN VIETNAM** Albert N. Garland, U.S.A. (ret.)	$3.50
08365-8	**HITLER MUST DIE!** Herbert Molloy Mason, Jr.	$3.95
08810-2	**LITTLE SHIP BIG WAR: THE SAGA OF DE343** Commander Edward P. Stafford, U.S.N. (ret.)	$3.95
08253-8	**WE LED THE WAY** William O. Darby and William H. Baumer	$3.50
08474-3	**GUADALCANAL** Edwin P. Hoyt	$3.50
08513-8	**PANZER ARMY AFRICA** James Lucas	$3.50
08682-7	**THE END OF THE JAPANESE IMPERIAL NAVY** Masanori Ito	$3.50
07737-2	**48 HOURS TO HAMMELBURG** Charles Whiting	$2.95
07733-X	**THE INCREDIBLE 305th** Wilbur Morrison	$2.95
08066-7	**THE KAMIKAZES** Edwin P. Hoyt	$3.50
07618-X	**KASSERINE PASS** Martin Blumenson	$3.50
08624-X	**NIGHT DROP: THE AMERICAN AIRBORNE INVASION OF NORMANDY** S.L.A. Marshall	$3.95

Available at your local bookstore or return this form to:

JOVE
THE BERKLEY PUBLISHING GROUP, Dept. B
390 Murray Hill Parkway, East Rutherford, NJ 07073

Please send me the titles checked above. I enclose _____. Include $1.00 for postage and handling if one book is ordered; add 25¢ per book for two or more not to exceed $1.75. CA, IL, NJ, NY, PA, and TN residents please add sales tax. Prices subject to change without notice and may be higher in Canada. Do not send cash.

NAME_____

ADDRESS_____

CITY_____ STATE/ZIP_____

(Allow six weeks for delivery.)

★ VIETNAM ★

__ **Dau** Ed Dodge/0-425-09552-2/$3.50
The <u>real</u> Vietnam War. Not the war of politicians, generals,
reporters, cameramen, protestors, or historians. The war
of the men who went through it all. And now tell it
all—like is was never supposed to be told.

__ **Taxi Dancer** Joe T. Heywood/0-425-07966-X/$3.50
They were the last breed of fighter jocks, an elite corps
of jet pilots who flew the controversial bombing missions
over North Vietnam. And here is their story.

__ **The Berets** W. E. B. Griffin/0-515-09020-4/$3.95
They were the chosen ones. Never before had the United
States given so select a group such punishing preparation.
Now they were heading for their ultimate test of skill and
nerve...Vietnam. Book V of the <u>Brotherhood of War</u> series.

__ **The Generals** W. E. B. Griffin/0-515-08455-7/$3.95
They were the leaders, men who made the decisions that
changed the outcome of battles and the fate of continents.
Now they lead America's finest against her most relentless
enemy deep in the jungles of Southeast Asia. Book VI of
the <u>Brotherhood of War</u> series.

Prices may be slightly higher in Canada.

True accounts of Vietnam.

From the men who saw it all.
Did it all. And lived to tell it all.

_____ **Phantom Over Vietnam: Fighter Pilot, USMC**
John Trotti
0-425-08084-4/$3.50

_____ **Survivors: American POWs in Vietnam**
Zalin Grant
0-425-09689-0/$3.50

_____ **The Killing Zone: My Life in the Vietnam War**
Frederick Downs
0-425-08844-8/$3.95

_____ **Aftermath**
Frederick Downs
0-425-09177-5/$3.50

_____ **Nam**
Marc Baker
0-425-09571-1/$3.95

_____ **Infantry in Vietnam: Small Unit Actions in the Early Days 1965-66**
Edited by LTC Albert N. Garland USA (Ret)
0-515-08054-3/$3.50

_____ **Brothers: Black Soldiers in the Nam**
Stanley Goff and Robert Sanders
0-425-09174-0/$3.50

_____ **Inside the Green Berets**
Col. Charles M. Simpson III
0-425-09146-5/$3.50

_____ **The Grunts**
Charles R. Anderson
0-425-09154-X/$3.50

_____ **The Tunnels of Cu Chi**
Tom Mangold and John Penycate
0-425-08951-7/$3.95

_____ **And Brave Men, Too**
Timothy S. Lowry
0-425-09105-8/$3.95

Available at your local bookstore or return this form to:

BERKLEY
THE BERKLEY PUBLISHING GROUP, Dept. B
390 Murray Hill Parkway, East Rutherford, NJ 07073

Please send me the titles checked above. I enclose _____. Include $1.00 for postage and handling if one book is ordered; add 25¢ per book for two or more not to exceed $1.75. CA, IL, NJ, NY, PA, and TN residents please add sales tax. Prices subject to change without notice and may be higher in Canada. Do not send cash.

NAME_____

ADDRESS_____

CITY_____ STATE/ZIP_____

(Allow six weeks for delivery.)   424